# *Walk*

# in magnificent

# **Snowdonia**

i

# By the same Author

Walk in the beautiful Conwy Valley

Walk Snowdonia
     trackways
     packhorse trails
     Roman roads

Walk in the romantic Vale of Ffestiniog

Walk Snowdonia Peaks

*Walk*

# in magnificent

# **Snowdonia**

## Ralph Maddern

FOCUS PUBLICATIONS · WINDSOR

© Ralph Maddern

First published in Great Britain 1979
Second edition 1981
Third edition 1986
Fourth edition (revised) 1990

Focus Publications Ltd
9 Priors Road
Windsor
Berkshire SL4 4PD

ISBN 1 872050 02 6

Printed in Great Britain by
Grosvenor Press (Portsmouth) Ltd.

# The Walks

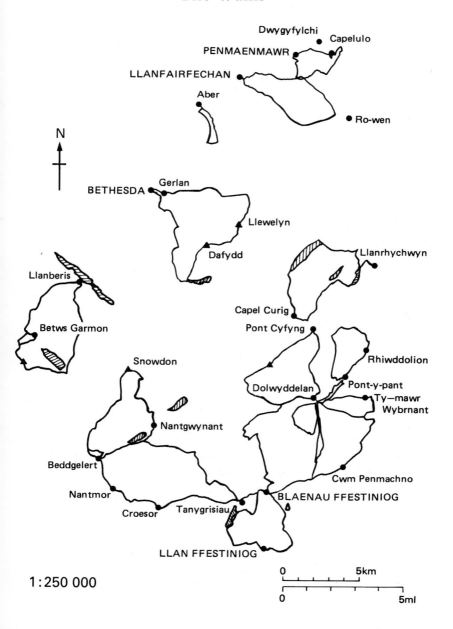

1:250 000

# Illustrations by June Jackson

# Outline Portraits

# Contents

vii

# Compass Bearings

## Pedometer Readings

### and Snowdonia

Accuracy of position and direction is ensured by combining two kinds of measurement: distance registered by a pedometer, and direction recorded by a compass.

A pedometer reading may be taken to be correct to the nearest one-tenth of a kilometre or one hundred metres: 1.7km is within the range 1.65km to 1.75km, 1650 metres to 1750 metres,

A compass bearing of 080° can be accepted as lying within the arc 075° to 085°.

To determine a bearing, hold a hand compass in a horizontal position and allow the needle to steady. Turn the circle graduated in degrees until the N/S marking – 0°/360° to 180° – lies exactly beneath the needle.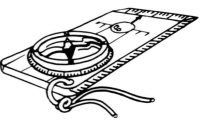

If a bearing in this text is to be followed move the base platform until its centre line registers the required reading on the graduated circle.

If the bearing of an object from a position on the ground is required, move the base platform until its centreline is aligned with the object. Read the object's bearing on the graduated circle.

If seeking a bearing from an Ordnance Survey map in order to follow a direction on the ground,

★ place the centre of the graduated circle on the map position from which the bearing is to be taken

★ move the grid lines of the graduated circle to coincide with those of the OS map

★ Align the base platform's centreline on the map with the object whose bearing is required and read the bearing on the graduated circle.

# Welsh

Place names in Wales are fascinating because of the descriptions they offer of their locations. That is why interpretations are given where this is possible. Understanding what the name means is often a major clue to knowing the place itself. Pronunciation can be quite difficult for a non-Welsh speaker but it is worth trying to get the right sound. The main sounds, where these differ from English, are set out below.

a     as in *are*

c     always hard as in *car*

Ch   as in the Scottish *loch*

e     "ay" as in *say*

f     as in the English *"v"*

Ff   as in the English *"f"*

g     always hard as in *give*

Ll   place the tongue to form "l" but emit a passage of air through the tongue to merge with the following letter

r     rolled more strongly than in English

Rh   both the "r" and the "h" are pronounced

Th   as in *both*

Dd   also "th" but as in *this*

u     "i" as in *it* or "ee" as in *feet*

w    "oo" as in roost (Llanrwst = Llanroost) – it also works like the English "w"

y     "u" as in *fun* or "ee" as in *feet* or "i" as in *pin* (you have to listen)

J, K, Q, V, X and Z do not appear in Welsh as these sounds are conveyed by other letters or diphthongs.

As with some Welsh poetry the evocative quality in the term *critch-cratch* eludes adequate representation in English. *Critch-cratch* refers to a gate hung in a U or V-shaped enclosure and is, therefore, impassable to stock animals. It is sometimes known as a "kissing gate".

*Critch-cratch* seems much more illustrative and evocative.

**Countryside** COMMISSION

### YOUR RIGHTS OF WAY ARE

Public footpaths – on foot only. *Sometimes waymarked in yellow*

Bridleways – on foot, horseback and pedal cycle. *Sometimes waymarked in blue*

Byways (usually old roads), most "Roads Used as Public Paths" and, of course, public roads – all traffic.

*Use maps, signs and waymarks. Ordnance Survey Pathfinder and Landranger maps show most public rights of way.*

### ON RIGHTS OF WAY YOU CAN

Take a pram, pushchair or wheelchair if practicable

Take a dog (on a lead or under close control)

Take a short route round an illegal obstruction or remove it sufficiently to get past.

### YOU HAVE A RIGHT TO GO FOR RECREATION TO

Public parks and open spaces – on foot

Most commons near older towns and cities – on foot and sometimes on horseback

Private land where the owner has a formal agreement with the local authority.

**IN ADDITION** you can *use* by local or established *custom or consent*, but ask for advice if you're unsure:

Many areas of open country like moorland, fell and coastal areas, especially those of the National Trust, and some commons

Some woods and forests, especially those owned by the Forestry Commission

Country Parks and picnic sites

Most beaches

Canal towpaths

Some private paths and tracks.

*Consent sometimes extends to riding horses and pedal cycles.*

### FOR YOUR INFORMATION

County councils and London boroughs maintain and record rights of way, and register commons

Obstructions, dangerous animals, harassment and misleading signs on rights of way are illegal and you should report them to the county council

Paths across fields can be ploughed, but must normally be reinstated within two weeks

Landowners can require you to leave land to which you have no right of access

Motor vehicles are normally permitted only on roads, byways and some "Roads Used as Public Paths"

Follow any local bylaws.

### AND, WHEREVER YOU GO, FOLLOW THE COUNTRY CODE

Enjoy the countryside and respect its life and work

Guard against all risk of fire

Fasten all gates

Keep your dogs under close control

Keep to public paths across farmland

Use gates and stiles to cross fences, hedges and walls

Leave livestock, crops and machinery alone

Take your litter home

Help to keep all water clean

Protect wildlife, plants and trees

Take special care on country roads

Make no unnecessary noise.

*This Charter is for practical guidance in England and Wales only. Fuller advice is given in a free booklet "Out in the country" available from Countryside Commission Publications Despatch Department, 19–23 Albert Road, Manchester M19 2EQ.*

Published with grant aid from the

**Cefn Gwlad**

## DYMA EICH HAWLIAU TRAMWY

Llwybrau cyhoeddus – ar droed yn unig. *Fe'u dynodir weithiau â'r lliw melyn*
Llwybrau ceffyl – ar droed, ar gefn ceffyl neu feic. *Fe'u dynodir weithiau â'r lliw glas*
Cilffyrdd (hen ffyrdd fel arfer), y mwyafrif o "Ffyrdd a Ddefnyddir fel Llwybrau Cyhoeddus" ac wrth gwrs, ffyrdd cyhoeddus – pob trafnidiaeth. Defnyddiwch fapiau, arwyddion a mynegbyst. *Dangosir y mwyafrif o hawliau tramwy cyhoeddus ar fapiau Pathfinder a Landranger yr Arolwg Ordnans.*

## LLE BO HAWLIAU TRAMWY GALLWCH

Fynd â phram, coets gadair neu gadair olwyn os yw'n ymarferol
Fynd â chi (ar dennyn neu dan reolaeth glos)
Gymryd ffordd fer o gwmpas rhwystr anghyfreithlon neu ei symud ddigon i fynd heibio iddo.

## MAE GENNYCH HAWL I FYND I HAMDDENA

Mewn parciau cyhoeddus a mannau agored – ar droed
I'r mwyafrif o diroedd comin gerllaw hen drefi a dinasoedd – ar droed ac weithiau ar gefn ceffyl
Ar dir preifat lle mae gan y perchennog gytundeb ffurfiol â'r awdurdod lleol.

## YN OGYSTAL gallwch *ddefnyddio* trwy arfer neu ganiatâd *lleol neu sefydlog* ond gofynnwch am gyngor os ydych yn ansicr:

Llawer darn o dir agored fel rhostir, bryniau a'r arfordir, yn enwedig rhai'r Ymddiriedolaeth Genedlaethol a rhai tiroedd comin.
Rhai coedlannau a choedwigoedd, yn enwedig y rhai sy'n eiddo i'r Comisiwn Coedwigaeth
Parciau Gwledig a safleoedd picnic
Mwyafrif ein traethau
Llwybrau ymyl y camlesi
Rhai llwybrau a thraciau preifat
*Estynnir caniatâd weithiau i gynnwys mynd ar gefn ceffyl neu feic.*

## ER GWYBODAETH I CHI

Mae cynghorau sir a bwrdeisdrefi Llundain yn cynnal a chofnodi hawliau tramwy, ac yn cofrestru tir comin
Mae rhwystrau, anifeiliaid peryglus, erledigaeth ac arwyddion camarweiniol yn anghyfreithlon a dylech roi gwybod i'r cyngor sir amdanynt
Gellir aredig llwybrau sy'n croesi caeau, ond rhaid eu hadfer o fewn pythefnos fel arfer
Gall tirfeddiannwyr fynnu eich bod yn gadael tir lle nad oes gennych hawl mynediad
Ni chaniateir moduron fel arfer ond ar ffyrdd, cilffyrdd a rhai "Ffyrdd a Ddefnyddir fel Llwybrau Cyhoeddus"
Parchwch unrhyw is-ddeddfau lleol

## A, LLE BYNNAG YR EWCH, DILYNWCH Y RHEOLAU CEFN GWLAD

Mwynhewch y wlad a pharchwch ei bywyd a'i gwaith
Gwyliwch rhag holl beryglon tân
Caewch bob llidiard
Cadwch eich cŵn dan reolaeth glos
Cadwch at lwybrau cyhoeddus wrth groesi tir amaethyddol
Defnyddiwch lidiardau a chamfeydd i groesi ffensys, gwrychoedd a waliau
Gadewch lonydd i anifeiliaid, cnydau a pheiriannau
Ewch â'ch sbwriel adre gyda chi
Helpwch gadw pob dŵr yn lân
Cymerwch ofal o goed, creaduriaid a phlanhigion gwyllt
Byddwch yn ofalus iawn ar ffyrdd gwledig
Peidiwch â chreu sŵn yn ddiangen

*Arweiniad ymarferol yw'r canllawiau hyn yng Nghymru a Lloegr yn unig. Ceir cyngor manylach o Swyddfa Cymru, Comisiwn Cefn Gwlad, Tŷ Ladywell, Y Drenewydd, Powys SY16 1RD.*

Cyhoeddwyd gyda chymorth ariannol

## The pathmakers of Eryri

Approaching these mountains from afar one has the impression of an arrangement contrived by a giant sculptor. Rising from their surroundings in compact formation, each shape blends into a weathered totality which draws attention and arouses curiosity.

Entering this sanctuary the early Celts established their settlements on the higher ground which offered security from enemies. They grazed animals on the slopes and cultivated plots round their huts. Metal merchants tramped between the settlements. These traders specialised in copper, tin, zinc, lead and iron. Business was done mainly by barter, so they had to deal also in hides, thread, cloth and grain.

Some of the ancient trackways must have been used by Roman legions but those conquerors preferred to build their own roads. Their technique was to establish strategically-sited forts and connect them by the most direct routes, using conscripted British labour to carry out the construction work.

The Roman roads would have aided the travels of the early Christian pilgrims, some of whom are immortalised as saints. They were practical men who sought assured water supplies. On their chosen spots they established settlements many of which bear their names.

Nordic, Saxon and Norman invaders thrust into the mountains along the trackways and Roman roads. Fortunately, not all of the routes they used are suitable for twentieth-century transport which prefers gentler grades along valleys rather than steep inclines over high passes.

Packhorse drivers of the pre-industrial age were not so inhibited. They took high passes in their strides. Their trails enabled isolated cottagers to receive a door-to-door service perhaps two or three times a year. Before the age of steam, oil and radio these men kept Snowdonians in touch with the wider world. That was when heat and light were made by burning trees and tallow candles. Then there was the explosion of the Industrial Revolution.

Landless labourers sank shafts beneath green pastures to mine metals for England's insatiable factories. Drovers urged herds of animals through the mountains to feed England's expanding population. Quarrymen split Welsh slate to cover the roofs of England's spreading cities. Snowdonians drained away from their homes to find work in strange lands.

Here on their holdings the farmers who remained continued their traditional lives, driving their stock to market, visiting neighbours on foot or pony along the old paths. Many of those holdings have now been subsumed in larger farms, but the paths remain. Their survival has been achieved by Eryri's special topography and their presence is marked by impressions in the earth.

So, we tread paths that could have been in use over a span of five thousand years. That makes them measurable against anything else that humans have made in these islands.

## Blaenau Ffestiniog

Approach from a high upland above the town. Let the eye rest upon the contrast between green moorland and a mountainside sculptured in blue-grey levels. Descend. If possible, use the track of an old tramway. Feel the enormous effort of human labour that has made this place. Two centuries of effort.

From the eighteenth century, when England plunged into her Industrial Revolution, Blaenau Ffestiniog became the site of one of the largest slate quarrying industries in the world, providing roofs for Britain's expanding population which more than quadrupled in the nineteenth century from nine to almost forty millions.

For at least half a century slate was transported to markets in Britain and abroad on farm carts through the Vale of Ffestiniog and thence in rowing barges down the Afon Dwyryd to the sea. In 1836 a horse-drawn railway was built, connecting Ffestiniog with Porthmadog, and in 1863 steam locomotives were introduced.

By the middle of the nineteenth century the companies had taken to mining, after the commercially accessible raw material near the surface had been worked out. This required a system in which men worked in groups of four, consisting of two rockmen who extracted the rock and two men who dressed the rough blocks and split them into usable slates. These groups of workers were dependent upon many others such as surveyors, miners, hauliers, platelayers and machinery attendants. Such a pattern of interdependence is a familiar feature of many mining communities but here in Wales there was a distinct cultural aspect.

For their mid-day meal, underground workers would gather in a sealed-off section of tunnel which they called *Y Caban*. Under a *Llywydd*, an elected chairman, they carried on wide-ranging discussions. On Monday and Tuesday the debate would be about sermons preached in the chapels on Sunday. A good Llywydd always sought to have the members of his caban probe the depths of meanings. For the remainder of the week the caban might turn to recitation, poetry, choral activities, the performances of brass bands. Each caban participated in quarry eisteddfodau. Adjudications were very exacting so each entry had to be well prepared.

The caban also served as a forum for political discussion and as a cell for organising the North Wales Quarrymen's Union. The quarry companies' profits, which were enormous for most of the nineteenth century, were appropriated by absentee owners who failed to invest adequately in the industry. Moreover, they pursued a practice of reckless extraction, removing rock from supporting walls, thereby considerably endangering the lives of quarrymen. The result was an increasing frequency of rock collapses, culminating in a great fall in February 1883 when more than six million tons of rock collapsed into the workings. Fortunately, the disaster did not occur during working hours.

Peak production was reached in 1889. The steady decline during the following years coincided with Britain's eclipse as the workshop of the world and when other sources of supply had entered the market. In 1900 the Quarrymen's Union was obliged to engage in a prolonged dispute over wages and working conditions. After three years the strike was lost and the quarrymen were forced back to work. Many migrated to other parts of Britain and abroad as the steep decline of the industry set in.

Nowadays, a small-scale operation is carried on, order books are full and there is a shortage of manpower. How Blaenau would welcome back some of those quarrymen who departed long ago taking their skills and intimate knowledge of the industry with them! Here is a massive monument to their lives and to their collective labour: raw, rugged, stark, but impressive – and strangely beautiful too.

# Walk 1

Blaenau Ffestiniog – Manod-bach – Llan Ffestiniog – Blaenau Ffestiniog: 18.4km, 11½ml.

Blaenau – Llan: 8km, 5ml.

From the Blaenau PO (00km; elevation: 244m, 800ft) walk E/SE along the A470 for 300m, fork left at the fifth turning left and continue round the massive boulder formation onto a path that winds up to a lane (0.4km). Turn right, follow the lane, bearing 150°, to a path (0.5km) and on to a T-Junction opposite a row of terraced cottages (0.8km). Turn right and continue to an old woollen mill (1.0km).

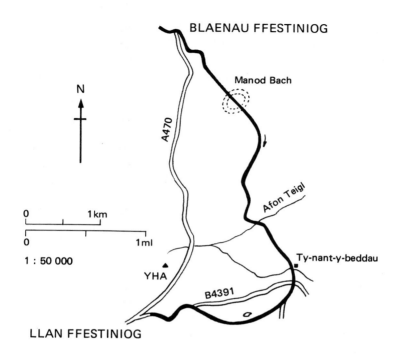

BLAENAU FFESTINIOG

Manod Bach

N

A470

Afon Teigl

0        1 km

0                    1 ml

1 : 50 000

YHA

Ty-nant-y-beddau

B4391

LLAN FFESTINIOG

If Blaenau's weather has been living up to its reputation one can stand on the little stone bridge and feel the massive power which this mill used to harness, tumbling down from Manod-bach, that rocky mass over which this route passes.

Turn left along the path by the bridge and begin the climb. Mark a point on the summit ridge with a general bearing of 140° and continue across the old trackway to the top of the mountain (1.9km, 1.2ml; elevation 473m, 1550ft).

Here is an incomparable viewpoint. On a bearing of 220° is Llan Ffestiniog, nestling in a wide expanse of the Vale of Ffestiniog. To the east is the bulk of Manod-mawr. In between the two Manods lies Llyn y Manod, well known for its trout.

Descend on 140°, cross a stream and join a path from Llyn y Manod at a wall gate (2.9km). Continue alongside a wall and through an opening 150m further on to a pair of ruins, Bryn-eithin (3.4km). About 50m beyond the ruins turn left (160°), follow a path across fields to wheeltracks (3.8km), turn right (220°) and continue down past the farmhouse Teiliau-mawr (4.0km, 2.5ml). Veer left (SE) from the farmyard, past the house Minafon on the left, across the Afon Teigl to a stile (4.4km) and up the hill to a wall stile (4.6km). Continue SE, crossing the Afon Nant Llynmorwynion and passing the farmhouse, Ty-nant-y-beddau, on the left. *Beddau* refers to graves. *Ty-nant-y-beddau*: house by the brook of the graves.

According to legend the graves, situated a few hundred metres eastward, are those of the men of Ardudwy – *Beddau Gwyr Ardudwy* – who, during the Middle Ages, went to Clwyd in search of young maids. They made their captures and set off for Ardudwy with their brides-to-be; but, apparently, they had not prepared themselves for the ferocious wrath of the men of Clwyd who pursued the raiders and cut them down here in this quiet upland. In confused distress the maids are alleged to have thrown themselves into nearby Llyn Morynion.

Continue up hill, across the B4391 to a stile, and on, bearing 200°, to a farm road (5.4km). Veer right and follow the road for 200m to a gate on the right where the wheeltracks bear 230°. After passing a small reservoir on the right (6.1km) veer to W and continue to a gated wall opening and wall steps (6.7km). Cross the field (300°) to a barn, follow wheeltracks to critch-cratch 1 and turn left along the B4391 to Llan Ffestiniog PO (8.0km, 5ml; elevation: 183m, 600ft).

# Llan Ffestiniog

Stiniog, as its intimates call it, was old when Blaenau was born out of the rocks at the head of the valley. This is part of the Welsh heartland, a place to which one could retreat and find safety. *Penffestin* literally means: a helmet. More freely translated it is a place with good defences, the mountains providing cover for ambush as well as a climate that puts the invader at a disadvantage.

Even so, invaders have trodden this ground. Owain Glyndwr in his fifteen-year independence struggle, was pursued by English forces from Llanrwst to Harlech over Ffestiniog in 1404. In the same century the Yorkist forces of King Edward IV pursued their enemies, the Lancastrians, over the same route after devastating Llanrwst in 1468. Almost two centuries later, in 1645–7, the Parliamentary army under Oliver Cromwell pursued Royalist forces by way of Ffestiniog and, in fact, Cromwell himself is known to have stayed at Dduallt, a house in the locality.

But such fracticidal activities did not affect the Welsh way of life. Go to the Pengwern Arms Inn and you will be in a house of old bards. At the end of the eighteenth century this inn was called *Yr Efail* – the smithy. It was kept by Dafydd Owen, a blacksmith, and his wife, Alsi. G.J. Williams records in *Hanes Plwyf Ffestiniog* how Huw Pierce, who lived in the nearby farmhouse, Pengwern, wrote many poems for Alsi. The blacksmith's daughter, Martha – *Martha'r Efail*, inspired even greater poetic imagination. Here is an *englyn*, a popular form of Welsh verse, from a Llanrwst bard, Absalom:

> Pob teithiwr fel gŵr geirwir – ni 'mwrthyd
> A Martha tra'i ceffir;
> Hon a gwyd ei bwyd a'i *bîr*
> Yn ddi-doll fe ddywedir.

> Every traveller like an honest man – will not leave
> Martha while she's available;
> She offers food and *beer*
> Which are incomparable.

At a time when the population was only sixty, Llan Ffestiniog had two other pubs besides Yr Efail. These were: *Y Ty-isa* – the lower house, and *Y Ty-ucha* – the higher house. This indicates the significance of the village as a traveller's rest and hostelry, but for locals Yr Efail was the centre for social activity. A funeral provided a great social occasion. After the deceased had been safely laid to rest the

19

mourners would go to Yr Efail, and each would put down on the bar counter a fee known as *shotri*. This might be sixpence or a shilling, depending on the status of the occasion, and it entitled each mourner to as much beer as he could hold. If anyone became drunk or disorderly he was put in the stocks which were situated in the cemetery, and left there overnight. The last pair of stocks was made by a carpenter, Dafydd Jones, in 1825. He was paid 25 shillings for the job but the iron work was sub-let to a William Roberts who was paid 18 pence.

The packhorse was then the main means for transporting goods. It had an important advantage over later forms of transport in that it did not require easy grades but could take the most direct routes over the mountains. In the late eighteenth-century Cadwaladr Jones, the shopkeeper in Llan Ffestiniog, supplied all his customers then numbering about seventy, with all their needs by driving his packhorse to Wrexham fair – just twice a year.

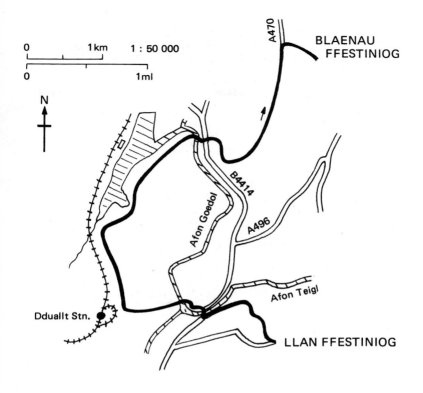

Llan – Blaenau: 10.4km, 6½ml.

From the PO (8.0km) continue SW along the B4391 for 100m and turn right (NW) by the Pengwern Arms. Follow the lane to its end and turn right to a gate (not the critch-cratch) on the left. Continue down to a gate on the right and turn left to a gate in the corner of the field.

Bear 350° across the field to a gate, continue to gates lower down passing a cottage on the left, NE then NW to a gate and turn right (N) to a barn and a path junction. Turn left (250°) and continue westward through a gate to a farm driveway and on to the A496. Turn sharp right and, 150m along the road, left along a driveway to a path 100m further on into the Nature Reserve, Coed Cymerau, where the Afon Goedol flows entrancingly through a delightful woodland.

Upstream a footbridge (10.3km) spans the river and beyond it the path winds up through the woodland to a plantation, sprouting amongst rugged textured rocks. Continue to a stile (10.8km), beyond which the Vale of Ffestiniog comes briefly into view, and after two more stiles (11.0km) veer to N, up the hill and across an old railway where the track of the restored Ffestiniog Railway is on the left.

Standing opposite the track one may be fortunate enough to hear an energetic locomotive puffing round the loop at Dduallt, just beyond the hillside. Then the incredible monster will appear, chugging up the track and sounding its whistle before disappearing into the tunnel towards Tanygrisiau.

Closed in 1946 and left derelict, the Ffestiniog railway attracted increasing attention from railway enthusiasts and others who found inspiration and purpose in the idea of restoring this engineering wonder, a once vital link between the Ffestiniog quarries and the sea at Porthmadog. Volunteers pooled their labour and in 1955 a section of the line was re-opened to passenger traffic using an original 1863 steam locomotive. The 'Ffestiniog miracle' has long since become a fascinating attraction for travellers from all over the world. Now, we can again ride the route of the rocking, rumbling, rattling slate trains from Porthmadog to Blaenau Ffestiniog and back again, enjoying magnificent views spanning the Vale of Ffestiniog.

Follow the track N to a point just beyond the end of the tunnel (12.6km) and veer right along a path that passes to the east of the Tanygrisiau reservoir, that shark-like stretch of water nurturing commendable rainbow trout. Sitting squarely on the shark's back is the Ffestiniog hydroelectric, pump-storage power station, going quietly about its non-polluting business generating power during peak consumption periods by using the pressure of water falling from Llyn Stwlan, a mountain lake secreted at the feet of those massive molars, the Moelwyns. During off-peak periods at night, excess power from the national grid is used to pump water back to Stwlan for further generation.

From a wall stile opposite the power station (14.0km) continue E to a footbridge and on to the B4814 (14.8km). Turn right and, at the second critch-cratch, 200m along the road, bear E and SE up and around the craggy outcrop south of Pen-y-cefn. Veer to NE down to a track that bears northward along the floor of Cwm Bowydd. Continue up through woodland south of the town, on past the square, over a footbridge (17.8km) that spans the railway and turn right to the Blaenau PO (18.4km, 11½ml).

# Walk 2

Blaenau Ffestiniog – Roman Bridge – Dolwyddelan – Blaenau Ffestiniog: 25.2km, 15.8ml.

Blaenau – Dolwyddelan: 14.5km, 9.1ml.

From the Blaenau PO (00km; elevation: 244m, 800ft) walk E/SE along the A470 for almost 200m, take the third turning left and continue N, following the quarry road as it curves eastward between hills of slate debris.

At 1.0km turn left across the route of an old tramway and follow the road NW. Before reaching a quarry building, about 500m further on, turn right and maintain a north bearing beyond the quarry workings to a gate and stile at the base of Ffridd-y-bwlch (2.4km). Continue uphill on a bearing of 350°, skirting the corner of a fence, to the left summit (2.7km; elevation: 473m, 1550ft). Here is a point to look back at Blaenau, nestling in its cwm, and see the quarries arranged as in a giant model.

Continue on 350° down to the A470 (3.6km, 2.2ml), cross the road and follow wheeltracks northward passing Moel Dyrnogydd on the left. One steps out onto an elevated space platform suspended on an S-bend (5.3km) above the upper Lledr. Below, on the right, the Afon Gorddinan

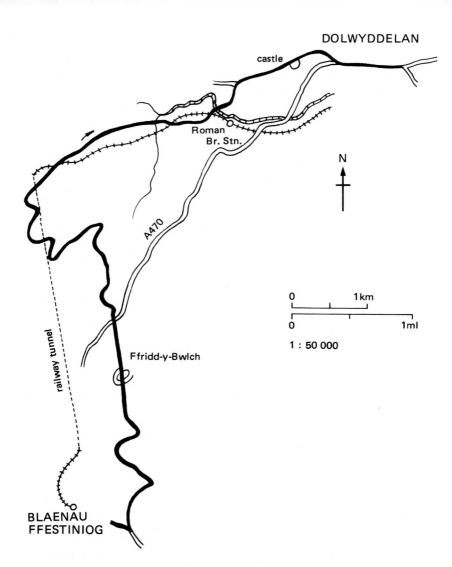

gushes down from Ffestiniog. On the left is the massive presence of Moel-siabod, while in the centre, on a bearing of 060°, is the keep of Dolwyddelan Castle.

Follow the track SW from the S-bend towards a miniature tower (6.3km) which is an air shaft of the railway tunnel far beneath. The track swings NE and winds northward to the tunnel mouth (8.2km). Continue NE through a railway culvert (8.6km) and on to the farmhouse Hendre (9.2km). At 9.5km turn right onto a path by a fence and continue E to a fence stile (10.0km), on past a cottage (Aber) and over a footbridge to a bridge that spans the railway. Turn left over the bridge and continue along wheeltracks to the farmhouse Gorddinan (11.0km).

At the end of the farm drive fork left over the railway and over *Pont Sarn-ddu* – black causeway – otherwise known as 'Roman Bridge', which spans the Afon Lledr. Rectangular piers carry massive stone lintels and long timbers across eight spans. An eighteenth-century map shows the road from Ffestiniog to Dolwyddelan crossing the river at this point.

Continue up the farm road for about 600m to the outbuildings of the farm Penrhiw (11.9km), turn right (080°) along wheeltracks and continue to Dolwyddelan Castle (13.0km, 8.1ml).

Approaching the castle at eye-level from the west, one may sense some of the romantic mystery of this hilltop sentinel. Here is a Welsh castle standing guard over the Lledr Valley and the route southward, that high pass (210°) which we crossed between Moel Dyrnogydd and Ffridd-y-bwlch – 'the Crimea' – as it came to be called in the nineteenth century because of the casualties it caused among vehicles and travellers.

The castle dates back to the end of the twelfth century, but just as the Welsh completed their work, almost a century later, it was taken from them, in 1283, by the English army under King Edward I. Here is thought to be the birth place of Llywelyn ap Gruffydd, the Welsh Prince of Wales whose head was carried to London in 1282 and exhibited on a spear with a wreath of ivy.

For much of the thirteenth century this was the royal residence of Welsh Princes. From the top of the keep one may enjoy a panorama of the enchanting Lledr Valley and of all the surrounding peaks where scouts would have been in clear view of this excellently-sited command headquarters.

From the north side of the castle follow the farm track E/SE down to the A470 (13.7km), turn left and continue to the village of Dolwyddelan (14.5km, 9.1ml; elevation: 143m, 470ft).

## Dolwyddelan

This large green meadow with its unfailing water supply and rich pasture must have attracted humans for thousands of years. *Dol* means meadow. *Dolwyddelan*, or colloquially, *Dol'ddelan*, refers to Gwyddelan's meadow. He was one of those sixth-century saints whose names are immortalised in the places they settled.

The Parish Church of St Gwyddelan is 100m SE along the Pentre-bont road from the post office. It dates from about 1500 when it replaced an earlier church 300m to the SW on a hill called *Bryn y Bedd* – hill of the tomb. From the

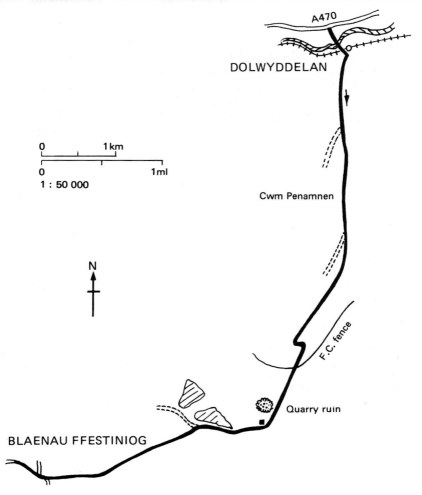

A470

DOLWYDDELAN

Cwm Penamnen

F.C. fence

0    1 km

0              1 ml

1 : 50 000

N

Quarry ruin

BLAENAU FFESTINIOG

post office walk 350m W along the A470 and turn left
through a pair of iron gates up to the cemetery. This is a
point from which Gwyddelan must have viewed his meadow.
On the right is the river, much as it must have been in his
day, but there is now the Llandudno to Ffestiniog railway
and the remains of slate quarrying. On the left is the main
road.

Nowadays, only one road passes through Dolwyddelan,
along the valley of the Afon Lledr, but when travel was by
foot and packhorse, this meadow was the nodal point in a

path network connecting many scattered mountain communities. Fortunately, these paths, traced out over thousands of years, remain for our use. They make the village an ideal centre for exploring this region of Snowdonia.


Dolwyddelan – Blaenau: 10.7km, 6.7ml.


From the PO (14.5km) walk SE to Pont y Llan (14.8km) which spans the Afon Lledr with three arches. After crossing the railway bridge fork left and, 100m further on, fork right to a forest road gate.

Follow the forest road southward, taking the left fork at 15.9km and again at 17.5km, rising steadily up Cwm Penamnen, once the habitat of sheep and wild flowers, now almost uniformly covered with the Forestry Commission's dark green. At 19.2km fork left, bearing 210°, along a path that zigzags up to a stile at the plantation boundary (19.9km, 12.4ml; elevation 473m, 1550ft).

We now have an expanse of elevated country at our disposal with the magnificent Machno Valley far below on the left. Continue S for 100m to a stile then bear 200° to a disused slate quarry and quarrymen's derelict barracks (21.1km). Stand under the huge beams of what was once the dining quarters and imagine what is was like when quarrymen lived here from Monday to Saturday, returning to their homes along mountain paths to spend Sundays with their families.

Continue W along the old quarry tramway which follows the southern shore of Llyn Bowydd reservoir. At 22.2km fork left from the track, bearing 245°, to a fence stile (22.6km) and continue to a wall ladder (22.8km). Follow the path down between two ponds to derelict winding piers (23.3km) and fork left 200m further down onto a path bearing 210°, which veers SW to W as it winds down to Blaenau Ffestiniog.

On reaching the A470 (24.8km) turn right to the Blaenau PO (25.2km, 15.8ml).

# Walk 3

Blaenau Ffestiniog – Tanygrisiau – Beddgelert – Nantmor – Croesor – Tanygrisiau – Blaenau Ffestiniog: 31.5km, 19.7ml.

Blaenau – Beddgelert: 15.5km, 9.7ml.

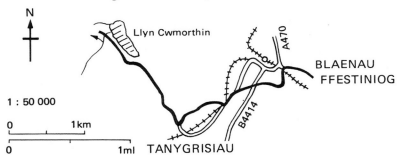

From the Blaenau PO (00km; elevation 244m, 800ft) walk NW along the A470 for 500m, turn left over a hump-backed footbridge that spans the railway and continue past the square to the second turning right. At the end of the street turn left then fork right along a tarmac path, cross the B4414 (1.1km), continue to the Tanygrisiau road (1.5km), turn left (SW) and, 200m on the right, turn right beneath the line of an old tramway (1.7km) to a path which bears 250°.

## Tanygrisiau

There was only a farm here in 1823 when quarry-master, Samuel Holland, took a lease and began building rows of houses for occupation by quarrymen and their families. The houses were sited close to the rocks and near the tramway. One can see the circumstances of its founding in the layout of the village: it clings tenaciously to the mountain massif rising westward.

Although linked to Blaenau industrially, Tanygrisiau has lived its own life and guarded its independent identity. A

29

school was established here in 1833 and a chapel in 1835, both built by volunteer labour. The village has fielded its own football teams, but in the matter of choirs and brass bands it has supported Llan Ffestiniog rather than Blaenau.

*Tan* means under, *grisiau* stairs. *Tanygrisiau*: under the stairs – which refers to the gradients of the mountain paths over which pre-industrial folk made their ways with their packhorse animals – they had to climb step by step.

Continue on 250° to a village road (2.5km), turn right and follow this old quarry track NW to the southern tip of Llyn Cwmorthin (3.3km). Take the left fork NW along the shore of the lake to a critch-cratch (3.8km), past a ruined chapel that once served this quarrying community, to critch-cratch 2 (4.5km). Veer to W then SW up the slope to the site of disused quarry buildings (4.8km), part of the old Rhosydd Quarries.

From the N-side of the derelict buildings bear 350° and continue northward passing to the west of Llyn Cwmcorsiog.

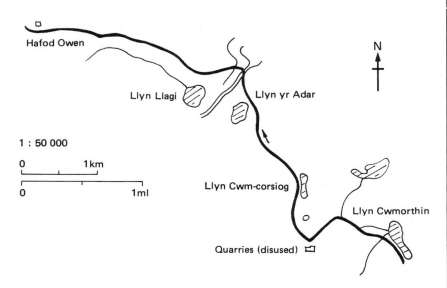

Hafod Owen

Llyn Llagi

Llyn yr Adar

N

1 : 50 000

0   1km

0   1ml

Llyn Cwm-corsiog

Llyn Cwmorthin

Quarries (disused)

30

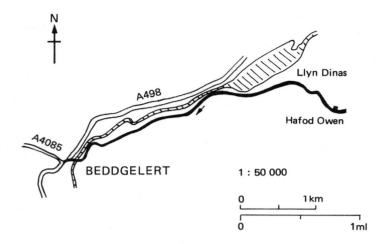

Cors refers to a bog; *corsiog*: boggy. *Llyn Cwmcorsiog*: lake in the cwm of bogs.

Veer to 330° from the ridge beyond the northern end of the lake, then 300° to the ridge SE of Llyn yr Adar. *Aderyn* is a bird; *adar* birds. Llyn yr Adar: lake of birds – a perfect name for this mountain lake with its central island, a superb haven for birdlife. Continue northward round the NE shore of the lake (7.0km), then NE to the ridge (7.3km) where, from an elevation of over 600m (2000ft), one can enjoy a sweeping view of the Nantgwynant Valley, and of the Snowdon massif which bears 330°.

After descending northward for 300m turn westward, passing Llyn Llagi on the left where there are remains of three pre-historic stone huts (map ref: 647484). Continue to a pair of cottages (10.1km), to critch-cratch 3 and a footbridge, and on to the cottage Cefn-gerhynt. *Cefn* means back, *ger* is near, *hynt* way. *Cefn-gerhynt*: back near the way. Indeed, the *hynt* is only 100m up the hill beyond critch cratch 4. Cross the council road (10.3km) and continue westward through critch-cratch 5 to a stile (10.6km), across a farm track (10.8km) to a wall gate (10.9km) and on through fields of wild rhododendrons to the cottage Hafod Owen (11.2km).

31

Continue NW through a rhododendron forest to a wall stile (11.4km) and down to a deciduous woodland beyond which one joins a path on the right (12.2km). Of all approaches to Beddgelert this, surely, is the most scenic: south-westward alongside the cool and serene Llyn Dinas, and the rippling chatter of the Afon Glaslyn, and through the profusion of wild rhododendron that climb far up the reddish-brown hillside. Copper is thought to be the nutrient that causes the brilliant blooming of the rhododendron in May. The mineral was mined here by a German company before the First World War and some of the shafts of what were known as the Sygun copper mines can still be seen.

The village itself does not appear until we enter it, crossing a footbridge to the west bank of the river and continuing to the PO (15.5km, 9.7ml).


## Beddgelert

Here is a story of continuity spanning the entire spectrum of history from the New Stone Age to the present day.

Discovery of stone and bronze implements (including a cache of bronze swords and daggers), remains of round huts, long huts, cairns and Iron Age smelting, confirm pre-historic occupation of the area.

The Romans left few remains but the location of their marching camp at Pen-y-gwryd, lower down the Nantgwynant Valley, clearly indicates their presence. Of course, the Romans did not neglect that strategic hill, Dinas Emrys (map ref: 606492), which had probably served as a fortress for centuries before the Roman period as it did for countless years after the conquerors had left.

Following the departure of the Romans there was an isolated Celtic community, among whom rose a priory, the oldest in Wales apart from the one on Bardsey Island. The monastery carried on an independent existence up to about 1200 when it came under the authority of the Abbey of Aberconwy. This was the period when the Parish Church of

St Mary was founded. Of the thirteenth-century Priory
Chapel there remains the north wall, including the doorway
to the vestry, two fine arches dividing the nave from the
transeptal chapel, and the east wall with its beautiful triplet
lancet window.

*Bedd* refers to a grave, *gelert* derives from a sixth-
century St Giler. This man's story is lost in the mists of time,
which was very convenient for the eighteenth-century originator of that other gelert, Llywelyn the Great's faithful
hound, whose fable can scarcely be missed in Beddgelert.
Less well known is the authentic historical presence of Wales's most popular hero: Owain Glyndwr (1359–1416).

At the beginning of the fifteenth century an air of violent conflict pervaded the British Isles. King Richard II had been overthrown in 1399 by an armed seizure of power and Henry IV was installed in his place. England was waging intermittent war in France, in Ireland and against the Scots. In 1400, Wales blazed into revolt when the Lord Marcher in North Wales, Lord Grey of Ruthin, sought to arrest Owain Glyndwr, ostensibly for refusing to respond to the king's summons for service against the Scots. Glyndwr escaped and succeeded in uniting almost the whole of Wales. Indeed, he was proclaimed Prince of Wales by his followers. He summoned a parliament and concluded a treaty with the King of France. But he was confronted by superior forces. During a period of defeat, about the year 1406, Glyndwr used, near Beddgelert, a cave which has been known ever since as Ogof Owain Glyndwr (map ref: 562478). A traditional story relates that supplies for the rebel chieftain were organised by the Prior of Beddgelert.

The cave is at the far end of Cwm Meillionen, in a rugged outcrop beneath the summit of Moel Hebog. From this vantage point lookouts could keep the entire surrounding areas under surveillance, as far as the peak of Snowdon, which rises magnificently across the valley.

The insurrection which Glyndwr led ended in defeat but after almost six centuries his memory remains undimmed – not least in Beddgelert.


Beddgelert to Blaenau: 16km, 10ml.

From the PO (15.5km; elevation: 46km, 150ft) walk E along the A4085, turn right over the bridge and immediately left to a footbridge spanning the Afon Glaslyn. Turn right (S) along the river path and continue through critch-cratch 6 (15.8km) to the footbridge 700m downstream. Here is the track of an old tramway which leads SE through two short tunnels, then a 300m tunnel (17.5km), beyond which is a stile (17.9km) and a council road (18.1km). Turn left to the village of Nantmor (18.3km).

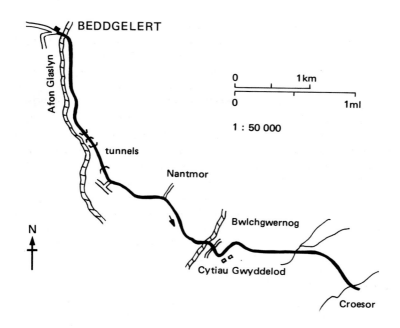

# Nantmor

A secluded haven in a leafy upland within close reach of the Pass of Aberglaslyn. This is how it may have appeared to those substantial citizens of long ago who built houses here.

*Ty-mawr*, otherwise known as *Capel Anwes* – chapel of ease – which dates from the fifteenth century, is the most notable house in the parish of Beddgelert (map ref: 610462).

*Hafod Garegog* dates from about 1600 when it replaced an earlier mansion. The site includes a mill, a cottage and a barn, all of the seventeenth century. (map ref: 604444)

*Gardd-llygaid-y-dydd* dates from the early seventeenth century and is said to have been the home of the mayor of Denbigh in 1623. (map ref: 605457)

Occupation in pre-historic times has been confirmed by the discovery of stone and bronze tools, and by the remains of stone huts and enclosures.

*Nantmor*, or *Nanmor*, derives from *Nant-y-mor*, gorge or brook by the sea, which washed up to this place in earlier times.

We take the old cart-track that once connected Beddgelert and Caernarfon with Maentwrog to the south-east. Continue SE from the village to a bridge spanning the Nanmor, and to Bwlchgwernog (19.9km) where a path bears S up a hill then veers E/NE. To the SE, about 200m, is the site of a pre-historic settlement known as *Cytiau Gwyddelod* – huts of the Irish (map ref: 614451).

Such is the rugged beauty of this wild terrain that one can imagine the Romans having departed yesterday – along the cart-track that leads SE to Croesor (22.2km, 13.9ml).

## Croesor

The renown of this village is associated with a man who lived here. Bob Owen Croesor was born in 1885 and left school at the age of thirteen to work as a farm labourer. When he was sixteen he began attending evening classes in Llanfrothen where a schoolmaster recognised an outstanding ability in arithmetic and demanded that he become a clerk. He worked in the Croesor Quarry office for thirty years, until it was closed in 1931, when he became unemployed. Every week he joined the dole queue in Porthmadoc but by then he was distinguished as a researcher, essayist, genealogist, bibliographer, and he was yet to find adequate outlet for his talents.

Bob Owen attributed his achievements to influences he encountered at the quarry. The quarrymen were well-read and his colleagues in the quarry office commanded a wide range of skills, including mathematics and technology.

After twelve years' work Bob had saved £100 with which he intended to buy a motor-bike. But a carpenter in Llanfrothen had died leaving a well-stocked library. Bob spent all the money he had in buying the deceased man's library at one shilling a book.

When he married in 1923 Bob took his bride, Nel, to

Aberystwyth where they spent their honeymoon researching in the National Library. Bob regularly won essay competitions at eisteddfodau. His themes included histories of early settlers in the United States where many of his relatives had migrated. Students from universities such as Harvard and Yale would arrive at Bob's home, Ael-y-bryn, to consult him about material for their theses. He researched family trees and he maintained a voluminous correspondence with Welsh migrants, students and publications in America, Australia and elsewhere.

Whilst unemployed his passion for buying books never flagged. To his wife he said that if they were short of bread they could buy it at some other time, but if he missed a rare book he would have missed it forever.

After a year on the dole Bob was reported in the press, in various parts of the world, on the occasion of his being awarded an MA. Lecturers at Bangor University collected to buy him a cap and gown and they paid his fare to Swansea. But it was another year and a half before he got a job – albeit a temporary one, as an assistant librarian at Bangor University. However, his true vocation still lay before him. He discovered it by walking these ancient paths.

Walking was his mode of locomotion; climbing was his recreation. He knew every detail of the Cnicht, that peak nestling its heel against Croesor, and of the Moelwyns which divide this valley from Ffestiniog. He regularly followed the route of this walk, up through his old quarry and across to Tanygrisiau where he held evening classes with members of the football club. He walked to Trawsfynydd to conduct another evening class. He walked all over the area to research material.

Recognising the effectiveness of his lectures, the W.E.A. offered him a full-time post. Thereafter, he lectured on local history in towns, villages and hamlets all over Wales. He lectured in the four universities of Wales and to Welsh societies in English cities. He became a broadcaster on radio and television.

When he died in 1962 his personal library was found to contain 47,000 books. A coach with its seats removed was

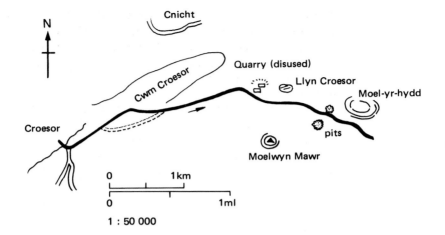

used to transport the books to the National Library in Aberystwyth. In an obituary in The Times of 2nd May 1962, Thomas Richard wrote of Bob Owen: "He was the most scientific genealogist of our generation in Wales".

Follow the village road SE for 200m, turn left (NE), continue past the farmhouse Croesor-fawr, fork right and, 150m further on, right again (E) onto a grass path that leads up the hill. Cross another path (23.6km) and continue upward (E) to join a quarry road (23.8km) which rises from the village road about midway between Croesor and Croesor-fawr. Here one may look back and see Croesor on guard at the entrance to its cwm and eye the Cnicht, that knight in shining armour, towering splendidly across the valley.

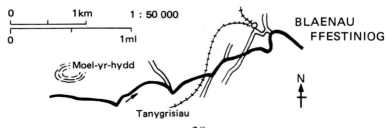

On reaching the stile at the western end of the Croesor Quarry building bear S for 50m then veer left to 100°. At the ridge, on the toe of Moelwyn-mawr, set a general bearing of 105° which takes one over a ridge of slate debris and between two well-sculptured quarry pits that add feature to the moorland landscape.

At the next ridge (26.5km), when the summit on the left, *Moel-yr-hydd* – mountain of the stag – bears 70°, set a general bearing of 120°. Continue downhill for about 600m then veer to E, to a point 20m north of a waterfall (27.4km), where there is a rugged descent eastwards to a council road (27.9km).

Turn left (NE) and continue to Tanygrisiau and the outward-bound path which leads back to Blaenau Ffestiniog (31.5km, 19.7ml).

# Walk 4

Dolwyddelan – Pont-y-pant – Dolwyddelan: 7.4km, 4.6ml.

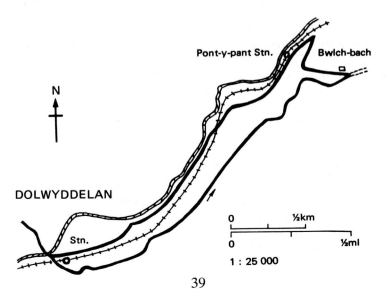

From the Dolwyddelan PO (00km; elevation: 143m, 470ft) walk SE to Pont y Llan (0.3km). After crossing the railway bridge fork left and continue for 100m where another left fork leads to a forest road stile (0.7km).

Beyond the profusion of slate quarry debris is an aerial view of Gwyddelan's meadow with the Afon Lledr meandering down the valley while the railway keeps unobtrusively under the southern ledge. Continue along the forest road to a path (3.4km) which turns sharp left (260°) and descends past the house *Bwlch-bach* – small gap (3.6km) – to a lane (4.2km) parallel to the railway. Turn left to Pont-y-pant railway station (4.4km, 2¾ml).

## Pont–y–pant

Not a village, scarcely a hamlet; really a few substantial residences scattered about the leafy slopes where quarrymen once tramped down to the railway station on their daily journeys to Blaenau Ffestiniog. Some of these dwellings, steeped in peace, quiet and seclusion, have been taken over by organisations devoted to outdoor activities.

*Pant* refers to a hollow. *Pont-y-pant*: bridge of the hollow. The bridge spans the narrows at the eastern end of Gwyddelan's meadow where the Afon Lledr begins a long and beautiful descent to the Conwy.

Follow the lane to the cottage Dolmurgoch (4.9km) then continue along the track which leads under a railway culvert (5.3km). There is now a pleasant stretch of river bank to Pentre-bont and Dolwyddelan (7.4km, 4.6ml).

## Walk 5

Dolwyddelan – Pentre-bont – Pen y Benar – Dolwyddelan: 7.4km, 4.6ml.

From the PO (00km; elevation: 143m, 470ft) walk SE to

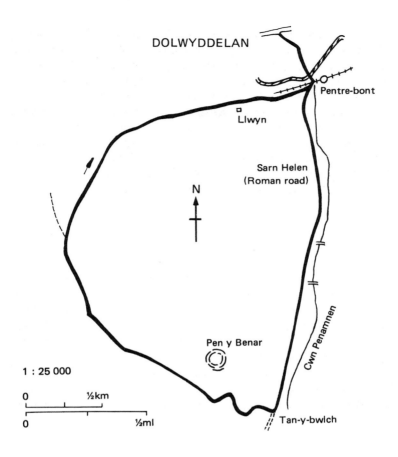

Pont y Llan, fork right after crossing the railway bridge and follow the route of a Roman road, now a tarmac farm road, through the hamlet of Pentre-bont which fills the mouth of Cwm Penamnen.

Continue to an old cottage, Tan-y-bwlch (2.9km, 1.8ml; elevation: 244m, 800ft). *Tan* means under, *bwlch* refers to a gap. *Tan-y-bwlch*: under the gap, which is the path one takes up the wall of the cwm. Turn right (300°) and climb into a dark tunnel provided by the overhanging plantation.

One plods through a half-light up a steep, ancient path embedded deep into the mountainside, until liberated at a fence stile (3.0km) under the brow of Pen y Benar (elevation: 429m, 1410ft). From the depths of the sombre plantation one ascends to the sudden, stunning sight of Snowdon and her sister peaks, Crib-y-ddysgl and Crib-goch, on a bearing of 300°.

Turn right, along the fence for about 30m, then left, down the valley (300°), through a gated opening (3.8km) and on, veering slightly right, to an opening between a wall corner and a *corlan-cerrig* (4.2km) – a walled enclosure for livestock. Follow the wall northward to a gated opening (4.5km), past a ruined cottage on the left; 200m further on fork right, bearing 020°.

Gwyddelan's meadow is again before us as we veer steadily eastward. At 5.9km fork right, alongside the wall on the left, to a stile (6.1km), then descend past the farmhouse Llwyn (6.5km) to Pentre-bont and Dolwyddelan (7.4km, 4.6ml).

# Walk 6

Dolwyddelan – Bwlch-y-groes – Cwm Penmachno – Dolwyddelan: 19.3km, 12ml.

Dolwyddelan – Cwm Penmachno: 10.1km, 6.3ml.

From the PO (00km; elevation: 143m, 470ft) walk SE to Pont y Llan, fork left after crossing the railway bridge and continue to the end of the village lane (0.6km).

The path is the old packhorse trail which follows the course of the Afon Bwlch-y-groes upstream, but a new forest road now scars the hillside and straddles the path from 0.9km to 2.0km where there is a gated opening. Continue uphill (SE) from the gate to a stile (2.7km) in Bwlch-y-groes where the high mound on the left (elevation: 455m, 1480ft) bears north. *Groes* refers to a cross or crossing; *bwlch* is a gap. *Bwlch-y-groes*: gap in the crossing.

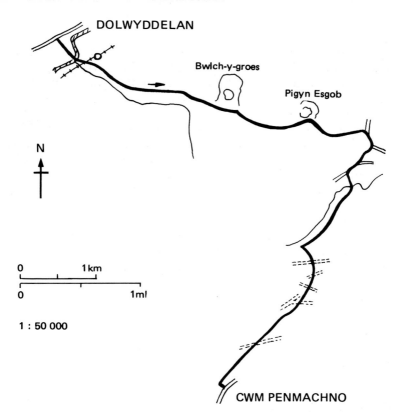

**DOLWYDDELAN**

Bwlch-y-groes

Pigyn Esgob

N

0         1 km

0                1 ml

1 : 50 000

CWM PENMACHNO

This is the high point (elevation 427m, 1400ft) on the old mountain path connecting Dolwyddelan with Penmachno and a traditional meeting place for people from those two villages. At least until the end of the eighteenth century villagers met here to compete in sporting activities. These were gatherings for men only, as the competitions were strictly tests for male prowess. There were tugs-of-war, wrestling matches and javelin throwing, and the location was sufficiently secluded to indulge in cock-fighting.

Turn right over the stile and continue on 160°, then 140° veering to E, skirting a plantation on the left, to a gated wall opening (3.6km). Continue on 120° alongside the wall on the right, through a wall opening, to the base of a rocky beacon known as Pigyn Esgob (3.8km). *Pigyn* means thorn, *Esgob* bishop. *Pigyn Esgob*: Bishop's Thorn.

Veer to E round the base of the 'thorn' and at 4.1km turn S and SE. Continue along a stream path to a gap in the plantation (4.4km), turn left (070°) and follow the path down to a council road (4.9km). Turn right and continue along the road for 300m to a forest road where the route diverges: left to Penmachno, right to Cwm Penmachno. Turn right (W) and follow the forest road for 30m, then veer SW down a path, crossing a forest road (5.7km), to a council road 50m further on. Turn right (W) and at 5.9km fork left, passing Plasglasgwm on the left.

After crossing the stream continue along the farm drive past *Dolgochyn* – red meadow (6.5km), SW to a forest gate (6.8km), up through the plantation to a forest road (7.1km) and turn right over a stile. On the right, across the Afon Glasgwm, is Blaen-y-glasgwm, a cottage which dates from the sixteenth century. *Glasgwm* refers to a green cwm. *Blaen-y-glasgwm*: end of the green cwm.

Continue to Tyddyn-du (7.5km) and bear SE to a forest gate 100m up the field. Follow the path SE, through the plantation across a forest road (7.7km) and on, bearing 170° then S, to another forest road (7.9km). Turn right and continue along the forest road, crossing another 100m further on, to a point where the forest road veers right (8.3km).

Follow the path SW across a forest road (8.4km) and on down through the plantation, over another forest road (9.1km) and SW to a stile (9.5km). Continue down the field to a footbridge (9.7km) and on to a village lane (10.1km, 6.3ml; map ref: 755476).

## Cwm Penmachno

Whatever may be said about the Cwm's end-of-the-world reputation this was a place of throbbing life. The beginning of summer was marked by a grand *gymanfa ganu* held in May. A choir of fifty voices was backed by a silver band, so-called because all the instruments contained silver and shone as brilliantly as the band's reputation. A performance was given in both of the chapels followed by repeat performances in Penmachno, Dolwyddelan and elsewhere in the district.

If the reputation of the choir and band was widely known, that of the Cwm football team was hardly less so. When the team returned from a fixture in the Conwy Valley or along the coast, Cwm turned out to welcome its heroes, lighting the way with candles in jars, hurricane lanterns and aladdin lamps.

Cwm's climax of the year was the children's eisteddfod held on Christmas Day. Tiny tots from the age of four would sing and recite on a platform before the chapel altar, and all Cwm was there to encourage them and enjoy their performance. A Cwm Christmas was a family gathering that included the whole village . . . .

And now the Cwm offers access to eternal blessings: immense peace; space to ponder the transient ways of humans; examples of nature restoring the consequences of human strivings.

The men who once climbed the steep slope at the end of the Cwm reported for duty at a quarry face; which was but yesterday in time's endless march.

Two millenia earlier, Roman legions strode this upland, taking the most direct route, of course – between the forts at Tomen-y-mur to the south and Caer Llugwy in the valley that now bears that name.

They marched for about two centuries . . . and disappeared.

They cleaved slate for about two centuries . . . and disappeared.

Nature covers their trails; heals their incursions; leaves impressions in the earth as messages through time of what once was.

Now, a walker may ascend to remoteness, imagining this vast area as one's own estate whose special gift is boundless scope for reflection.

Where legions marched, and slate was cleaved, thought may now sharpen its edge.


Cwm Penmachno – Dolwyddelan: 9.2km, 5.7ml.


From the point on the route at the corner of the village lane (map ref: 755476; 10.1km; elevation: 182m, 600ft) continue westward to a gate (10.3km) and along a path to stream fords about 200m north of the westernmost village houses at Glanaber Terrace. Bear 250° up the stream path which is adjacent to a plantation boundary. At 11.2km, opposite a stile where the stream bed widens, veer to 280° and continue across the hill for 500m, then bear 250° over the ridge to a mound of slate debris (12.6km) beyond which is the derelict barrack building where quarrymen once lodged during their working week.

From the eastern end of the barrack (12.7km) bear 010° up and over the slate heaps, past a quarry pit (13.0km), then continue on 020° across open moorland to stiles at the boundary of a plantation that envelops Cwm Penamnen (13.9km). Follow the quarrymen's path down through the plantation, over two forest roads, to a forest road junction (15.5km). Turn right and continue northward.

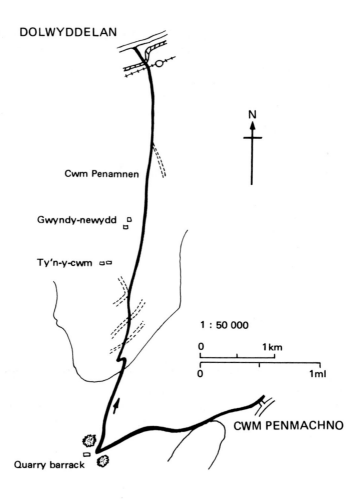

DOLWYDDELAN

N

Cwm Penamnen

Gwyndy-newydd

Ty'n-y-cwm

1 : 50 000

0           1 km

0           1 ml

CWM PENMACHNO

Quarry barrack

On the left, through a break in the trees, one sees *Ty'n-y-cwm* – house in the cwm – and, further along, *Gwyndy-newydd* – new white house – *new* because it once replaced a seventeenth-century house.

The forest road leads down to Pont y Llan and Dolwyddelan (19.3km, 12ml).

# Walk 7

Dolwyddelan – Ty-mawr Wybrnant – Dolwyddelan: 10.8km, 6¾ml.

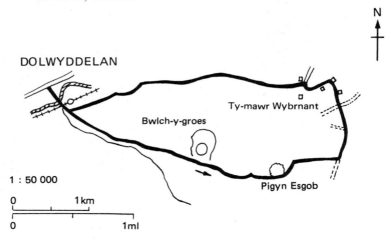

From the Dolwyddelan PO (00km) proceed as in Walk 6 to Pigyn Esgob (3.8km). After veering left round the base of the 'thorn' continue on a bearing of 050° for about 350m to a wall opening and then eastward along it to a council road (5.0km). Turn left and follow the road northward to Ty-mawr Wybrnant (6.6km, 4.1ml).

The significance of the life which began here extends beyond Wales, beyond Britain; is reflected in today's world and will be, presumably, in tomorrow's.

The year 1588. The Spanish Armada, prepared over many years and supported by Europe's most powerful rulers, sailed on its mission of conquest, the purpose of which was to reverse the Reformation of half a century earlier. Within this island every measure had to be taken to counter Spanish, or Catholic, influence if independence was to be safeguarded.

Bishop William Morgan, who was born in this house, had been working at his Welsh translation of the Bible for more than ten years, a labour of devotion that may be seen as part of the Reformation movement. By sanctioning publication of Morgan's Welsh Bible, the English government was adopting a measure against the external threat.

For generations of Welsh-speaking people, publication of the Welsh Bible in 1588 ensured continuity of their language; and through four centuries of cultural struggle there evolved a capacity to withstand the greatest challenge: the effects of a mass communication media and mass ownership of motor vehicles.

Ty-mawr Wybrnant resides in the care of the National Trust.

Fifty metres beyond a road gate in front of Ty-mawr a path veers left from the road behind the next farmhouse, Pwll-y-gath. Follow this path up the hill (W), across a forest road (7.0km) to the forest boundary (7.5km), where the path veering away right, bearing N then NW, leads to Ponty-y-pant.

Continue W with Bwlch-y-groes now on the left, the Snowdon peaks ranged magnificently ahead, while Moel-siabod presides above the deep green of Gwyddelan's meadow. Follow the path across heathered crags to a gate at the boundary of the next plantation (8.4km), on to a fence at the other side (9.1km), turn left and continue to an old quarry (9.5km).

We are walking along a quarrymen's path leading down to a forest gate (9.8km) and on to Dolwyddelan (10.8km, 6¾ml).

## Walk 8

Dolwyddelan – Pont Cyfyng – Moel-siabod – Dolwyddelan: 20.3km, 12.7ml.

Dolwyddelan – Moel-siabod: 10.3km, 6.6ml.

From the Dolwyddelan PO (00km; elevation: 143m, 470ft) follow the village lane NW up the hill for 100m, turn right through critch-cratch 1 and, 50m further on, veer left to critch-cratch 2 (0.3km). Continue to a forest road (0.8km), turn left (N), take the left fork at 1.2km and avoid all turnings to left or right until reaching the boundary forest gate (3.2km).

The track follows the route of an old packhorse trail across moorland at the foot of Moel-siabod, then winds NW down into the Llugwy Valley. On the descent there is a striking view of Cyfyng Falls (330°) cascading beneath Cyfyng Bridge which provides access from the A5 to the hamlet of Pont Cyfyng (6.1km).

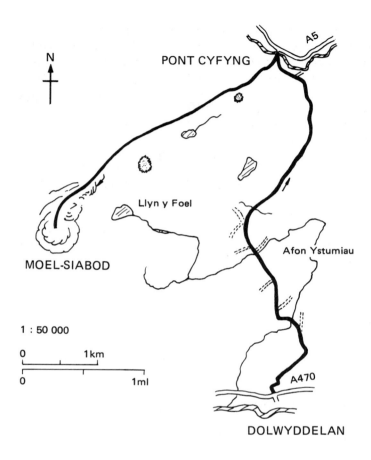

N

PONT CYFYNG

A5

MOEL-SIABOD

Llyn y Foel

Afon Ystumiau

1 : 50 000

0          1km

0          1ml

A470

DOLWYDDELAN

# Pont Cyfyng

*Cyfyng* means narrow. *Pont Cyfyng*: narrow bridge. It
nestles by the extended toe of Moel-siabod and was once the
settlement of quarrymen who worked in a pit up on the
mountain. The quarry was noted for a high-quality product,
the sulphur content of the slate being exceptionally low. In
addition to these terraced cottages the quarry company built
barracks on the mountain. Conditions there were said to be

more humane than in similar establishments at other quarries in that quarrymen could bring their families to live with them.

The quarry closed in 1940 and, since then, those arriving in Pont Cyfyng have come to view the mountain and not to carry it away.

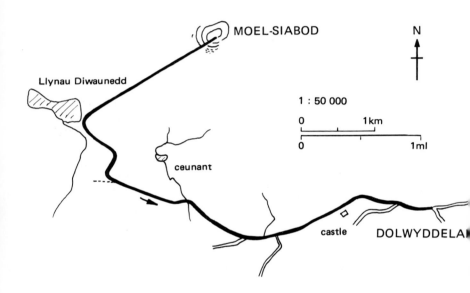

Turn sharp left (220°) up the tarmac farm road and continue for 400m to the farmhouse Rhos-y-goelcerth. Veer left onto wheeltracks and continue SW up the spine of the mountain passing a quarry pit on the left – the now silent workplace of the men of Pont Cyfyng.

If the weather is clear a magnificent view unfolds on both sides of the mountain spine: the Snowdon massif to the right, the Conwy Valley to the left, while faraway to the north, beyond the smooth and jagged crests, is the sea. Far below is *Llyn y Foel*, lake of the bald top, that gives rise to the *Afon Ystumiau*, which means: meandering river. It drains the moorlands which we traversed beneath the feet of Siabod.

After several false summits the climber enters the region which has possibly been North Wales's longest serving weather beacon. The visibility of Siabod's peak has long been regarded by people living in the region of these mountains as the surest sign of weather intentions.

If mist shrouds the peak (10.3km, 6.6ml; elevation: 872m, 2860ft), signalling unsettled weather, a bearing of 240° takes one down the moutain spine to the western tip of Llynau Diwaunedd, a pair of lakes sunk in a pair of mountain pits.

Join the course of the stream tumbling down from Siabod in its final flow to Llynau Diwaunedd and turn left to the forest road at the eastern end of the lakes (13.3km). Follow the forest road SE then SW to a path on the left (14.2km) and bear 160° to join the route from Nantgwynant (14.7km). Continue to the ford at the *ceunant* – the ravine (15.8km) – and to Ffridd (16.7km). A path 50m further on in front of the cottage leads down to Roman Bridge. Continue along the farm road past Ffridd Newydd (17.0km) and Pen-y-rhiw (17.4km).

Follow the path eastward to Dolwyddelan Castle. (see Walk 2).

Continue down to the A470 and turn left to Dolwyddelan (20.3km, 12.7ml).

# Walk 9

Pont-y-pant – Rhiwddolion – Bryn-gefeilia – Pont-y-pant:
12.5km, 7.8ml.

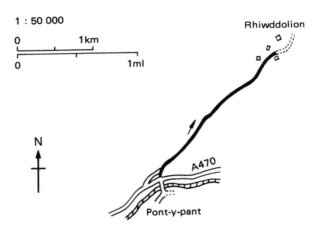

From the Pont-y-pant (00km; map ref: 756538; elevation: 145m, 475ft), the bridge which spans the Afon Lledr,
cross the A470, climb the slate steps and continue straight up
the hill to a stile (0.1km) by a farm road. Turn right (NE)
and follow the tramp of the legionaries along *Sarn Helen* –
Helen's way. She was a Roman official's wife who, so the
story goes, persuaded the reluctant British to expend fully of
their labours in building Roman roads.

Those who pass this way in summer may enjoy a wild
rock garden in bloom, for here is a profusion of heathers,
pink and white, sharing space with the hardy gorse, but
leaving room for bilberry, harebell and blackberry in blos-
som: all compactly draped round mellow rocks and discreet-
ly exuding delicate scents. With senses primed one comes
upon a deserted village (2.6km, 1.6ml; elevation: 230m,
750ft).

## Rhiwddolion

This was home for a quarryman tramping up the path from Pont-y-pant. The time might be six o'clock, and if the evenings were lengthening, there was a chance to do an hour's work outside before the evening meal. It was a place where a man could rent a smallholding, as well as earn a wage in a quarry.

Rising before five each morning, he would tramp with his neighbours down the path to the railway station at Pont-y-pant to catch a train to Ffestiniog where work started at seven. In high summer he would probably be up by three to do a stint at harvesting before setting out for the quarries.

Once a week his wife would carry her baskets of eggs and butter down Sarn Helen – known locally as Sarn Lleng –

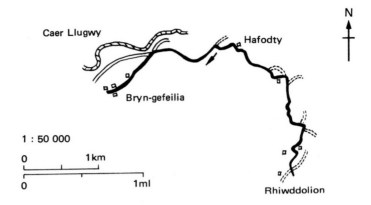

Caer Llugwy

Hafodty

Bryn-gefeilia

1 : 50 000

0        1 km

0                    1 ml

Rhiwddolion

to market in Betws-y-coed. When she had disposed of her produce she would pack her baskets with provisions and trudge back up the path to this secluded village.

The children went to school in the chapel, which served as a school on weekdays and a Sunday School on Sundays.

This little community was dispersed when the great depression of the early 1930s extinguished practically all quarrying in Ffestiniog.

Fork left (N) from the Roman road (2.6km) past a ruined terrace, then veer right across a stream to the village green. Turn left (310°) from the green, re-cross the stream and join a path by a pair of ruined cottages. Turn right (050°) and continue past the converted chapel to a stile at the edge of a plantation (3.2km).

Follow the path NE to a forest road (3.3km), turn left (NW), take the left fork 100m further on and fork left (N) again at 4.1km. Turn left at 4.3km and, 50m further on, fork, right onto a path bearing 300° past a ruined cottage on the left. Veer left round the cottage and through the plantation on a bearing of 230°/250°, then veer right to 290°/320°, continue across a forest road (4.6km) and on over a stream to a farm boundary (4.7km). (Alternatively, one may follow the forest road from 4.3km to 4.6km.)

Cross the field (300°) to a barn (4.9km), veer right and

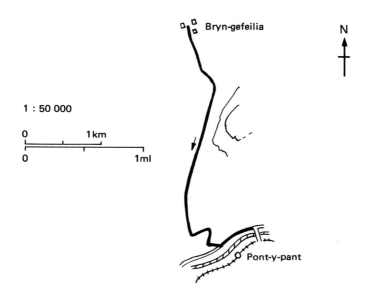

Bryn-gefeilia

N

1 : 50 000

0          1 km

0                1ml

Pont-y-pant

follow wheeltracks down the hill to a farmhouse, Hafodty (5.2km, 3.3ml; elevation: 230m, 750ft). Continue downhill (NW then W then N) to a forest road (5.6km), turn left (W) and take the next fork right (5.8km). At 6.6km cross a forest road and, 200m further on, fork left onto a path, bearing 220° from a council road.

Having descended into the Llugwy Valley we now begin to climb out of it using the route of a Roman road. But nearby, on the right, wedged into a U-bend of the Afon Llugwy, is the site of a Roman fort, Caer Llugwy (map ref: 747573). The site is thought to have been occupied from about AD 100 to AD 140 as part of a strategic network encompassing Snowdonia and extending southward and eastward.

Further along the track is the farmhouse Bryn-gefeilia (7.6km, 4¾ml; elevation: 183m, 600ft). *Bryn* means hill; *gefeiliau* refers to smithies. *Bryn-y-gefeiliau* – now shortened to *Bryn-gefeilia*: hill of smithies. The name applies to the surrounding area including the site of Caer Llugwy. Indeed, Bryn-y-gefeiliau may have originated with the Romans as excavation of Caer Llugwy suggests that industrial activity was carried on there.

From the west farmyard gate at Bryn-gefeilia follow wheeltracks S/SE to a gated opening at the farm boundary (8.7km). Continue across the moorland on a general bearing of 192°, passing near to the foot of Mynydd Cribar, a low ridge on the left facing the stately shape of Moel-siabod farther out on the right. Using the ridge of an ancient cob for part of the way follow the bearing to a gate (10.4km) where a change of bearing to 180° leads to a cart track (10.7km) which is about 200m west of a small reservoir.

About 500m further south turn left (NE) and continue to a stile (11.4km), on round a barn to a gate (11.6km), through an old quarry, veering S to join a farm road opposite a farmhouse. Turn left (E) and follow the drive down to the A470 (12.0km) where the Pont-y-pant railway station is directly across the river.

Turn left and continue to Pont-y-pant (12.5km, 7.8ml).


## Capel Curig

Anywhere along stretches of main road from Pont Cyfyng, up the Llugwy Valley towards Llyn Ogwen, and up the Nant towards Pen-y-gwryd, one is in Capel Curig. So elongated is this village, and so lacking in a centre, that it is not always easy to know where one is. The reason seems to be that when slate quarrying developed at the base of Moel-siabod, above Pont Cyfyng, inns were built nearby on the A5 to serve the needs of quarrymen. These inns were isolated from the place that could have served as the village's natural centre: opposite the church where the A4086 departs from the A5. When the village became a rendezvous for climbers, the inns became hotels and so the layout pattern was confirmed.

Climbing and sheep pasture are, of course, Capel Curig's year-round industries. But there is a part-time activity on which the latter is dependent and the former partially so. This is fox hunting. No packs of hounds. No sound of horns. No colourful riding habits. Simply a handful of shepherds who know where the lairs are and go out on foot with their dogs. They take about a hundred foxes a year.

## Walk 10

Capel Curig – Crafnant – Geirionydd – Llanrhychwyn – Cowlyd – Capel Curig: 22km, 13.8ml.

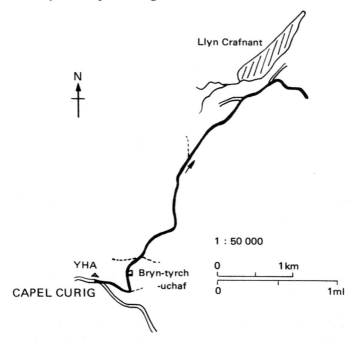

From the Capel Curig Youth Hostel (00km; elevation: 183m, 600ft) walk SE along the A5 for 200m, turn left along a farm drive to critch-cratch 1, continue to Bryn Tyrch-uchaf (0.8km) and follow the path to the left round the boundary of the house.

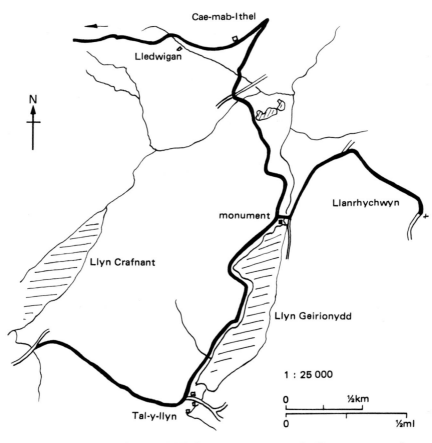

The route bears NE between an encircling range of weathered granite that plays with colours in harmony with sky and seasons.

One descends to a stile above the shore of Llyn Crafnant (4.5km; elevation: 206m, 675ft) resting serenely between mellow hills. *Craf* refers to garlic, *nant* to a gorge. *Crafnant*: gorge of garlic. Arrive in May and receive this wild plant's scent from the slopes of the gorge.

Follow the road NE for 400m to a stile on the right, bear E then SE up a mountain path to a forest road junction (5.8km) and continue to Tal-y-llyn (6.4km). *Tal* means end, *llyn* lake. *Tal-y-llyn*: end of the lake.

The path NE and N hugs the enchanting western shore
of Llyn Geirionydd. Ieuan Glan Geirionydd, which was the
pen-name of Evan Evans (1795–1855), wrote:

> Yr enwair ay y graean mân
>   I orwedd roed yn awr,
> Ac ar ryw lwydwyn faen gerllaw
>   Eisteddwn innau i lawr.
> Edrychwn amgylch ogylch ar
>   Y fangre unig fud,
> Heb sain na gwedd un dynol fod
>   Drwy'i holl ororau i gyd.

> The fishing rod on fine gravel
>   Was left there to lie,
> And on a greyish stone nearby
>   I placed myself to sit.
> I looked hither and thither on
>   This lonely quiet place
> Without human sound or face
>   In all this domain.

The scene from this bank must be very little changed even if the pines are now more profusely present than in the early nineteenth century. We may share the shapes, the sky-line, the contours, the lake itself, with bards across a time-span of almost two millenia.

Geirionydd has been a source of poetic inspiration from the beginnings of Welsh literature. It was here the sixth-century bard, Taliesin, lived. By the northern bank there is a stone monument (8.2km) which commemorates him, marking the spot that is said to be the true and natural venue for the *gorsedd*, the bardic circle of the National Eisteddfod.

From this point a diversion may be made, of 1.7km (1ml), turning right (E) to the tarmac then left (NE and SE), to the twelfth-century Parish Church of St Rhychwyn.

# Llanrhychwyn

This was the church of Prince Llywelyn ap Iorweth where he and his wife, Joan, came to worship before the Trefriw Church was built in 1230. In Llywelyn's time it was about half its present size forming approximately a double square around the font, which is said to be the oldest in Britain. With later extensions and alterations the church reached its present design in the eighteenth century. Services are held on the last Sunday in each month from May to September followed by a harvest festival.

From the monument (8.2km) follow the path northward to a stile (8.6km), fork right 50m further on and at 8.8km fork left (330°). Continue to a footbridge spanning the Afon Crafnant (9.3km) which supplies Trefriw, further down the valley, with power for its woollen mill.

On reaching the Crafnant-Trefriw road (9.4km) turn right, then left (020°), up a farm drive which swings sharply to SW at 10.0km, passing a farm cottage, Cae-mab-Ithel (10.3km). *Cae* is a field, *mab* is son. *Cae-mab-Ithel*: field of Ithel's son.

The track zig-zags uphill passing the farmhouse Lledwigan, lower down on the left. Bearing westward, ascend the steep slope to the north of *Allt-goch* – red cliff – across thick heather and marshy ground. When Llyn Cowlyd comes into view from the ridge (elevation: 490m, 1600ft) veer to NW and, while descending to the weir, let the eye range over the extent of Cwm Cowlyd stretching north-eastward to the edge of the Conwy Valley.

Scattered over the cwm are deserted cottages and farmhouses. Most are in ruins, having been abandoned as the industrial age developed. All provide evidence of a community that lived a self-sufficient life, isolated from the valleys and towns except for occasional visits to Trefriw or Llanrwst. At the lower end of the cwm, above Dolgarrog, are the ruins of Ardda, a village which served as a focal point for these interdependent, but independent, upland dwellers.

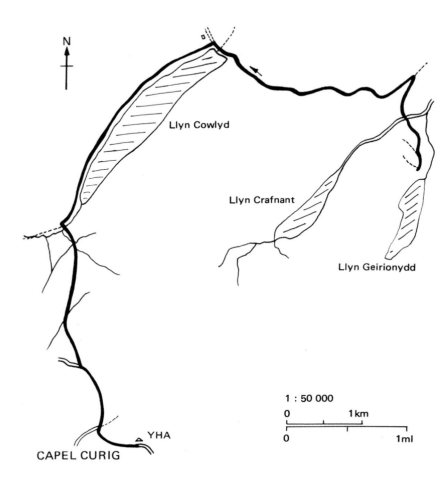

N

Llyn Cowlyd

Llyn Crafnant

Llyn Geirionydd

1 : 50 000

0              1 km

0                     1 ml

YHA

CAPEL CURIG

Now, there is only a pipeline carrying the purest of water to an unquenchable society.

On reaching the end of the weir (13.5km, 8½ml), turn left and follow the route of an old packhorse trail along the western shore at the foot of *Clogwyn-du* – black precipice. There are no boats or vehicles to sully the splendid isolation of this serene mountain lake, secure between its magnificent cliffs. If we ignore the low weir this is a sight we share with packhorse drivers and bards of former times.

Y llynnau gwyrddion llonydd, – a gysgant
    Mewn gwasgod o fynydd,
A thyn heulwen ysblennydd
Ar len y dŵr lun y dydd.


The still blue lakes – they sleep
    In a shelter of mountain,
And a splendid sunlight takes
A picture of the day on the surface of the water.


So wrote Gwilym Cowlyd (Gwilym Roberts, 1828–1904) who was born down the cwm at Tyddyn Wilym, Ardda. Like his uncle, Ieuan Glan Geirionydd, he sang of nature's perfection as he saw it all about him, this inspiring scenery providing the well-spring of his inspiration which brought him fame throughout Wales and beyond.

Ascend to the footbridge 300m beyond the southern end of Cowlyd (17.4km) to enjoy a final climax of this lakeland trek, then continue southward along the path to the A5 and SE to Capel Curig (22km, 13.8ml).


## Penmaenmawr

There was a village here, huddled against Wales's north coast, in the sixteenth century for it was mentioned in a play by Ben Jonson (1574-1637). In the nineteenth century, the leisured class favoured it as a resort because the mountain which gave the town its name sheltered the beach from the sun, thus preserving delicate Victorian skins. But its essential story is that of stone – as a glance at the steadily diminishing summit will confirm – and the quarry being worked above the town is only the latest example of an industry that can be traced back thousands of years.

In the later Stone Age, from about 2500 BC, Neolithic craftsmen worked the scree on the hillsides, especially above

Graiglwyd, to fashion stone axes, which then became commodities of trade at a time when Britain's earliest farmers needed to fell trees. Samples of these polished stone axes have been found at widely scattered sites in Wales and England. Identification is certain because rock from this end of the Snowdonian Mountains has a distinctive structure which is easily recognizable under microscopic examination. It has a hard and durable consistency throughout and its flaking property makes it easily workable.

From about 1500 BC the area was inhabited by Bronze Age people whose story is told in metal, pottery and burial chambers. Later, from about 300 BC, Iron Age farmers settled here.

In a circular walk one passes the site of Stone Age, Bronze Age and Iron Age cultures, as well as monuments of medieval times, and of the late eighteenth century when the Industrial Revolution initiated the inexorable movement of hill dwellers to the valleys and town.

# Walk 11

Penmaenmawr – Sychnant Pass – Capelulo – Penmaen-
    mawr: 13.5km, 8½ml.

This walk incorporates a route described in *Penmaen-mawr History Trail*, written by Dennis Roberts, and published as a leaflet in 1975 by the Penmaenmawr Historical Society.

From the Penmaenmawr PO (00km) bear W along the A55 for 200m, turn left (S) along a path between two chapels, take the next turning right (0.3km), then left, then right, to the lane Y Berllan. Follow the track bearing 140°, to the Graiglwyd Road (0.8km), turn right, continue for

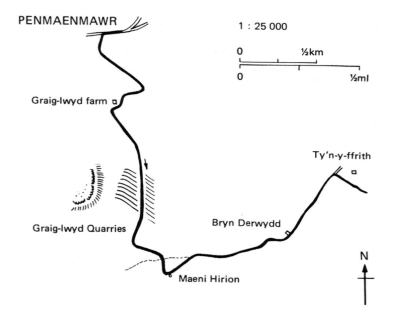

PENMAENMAWR

1 : 25 000

Graig-lwyd farm

Ty'n-y-ffrith

Graig-lwyd Quarries

Bryn Derwydd

Maeni Hirion

N

150m and fork left to critch-cratch 1 by Graiglwyd farm-house (1.1km). *Graig* means rock, *lwyd* is grey. *Graiglwyd*: grey rock. The farmhouse dates from the sixteenth century.

Follow the path southward up the hill across the site of a Neolithic stone axe factory which was discovered and exca-vated in the 1920s. This coastal cwm, situated close to a wide beach, provided easy access for Stone Age transportation by sea. Later, in the sixth century, a holy man named Seiriol is thought to have built a small church or cell hereabouts. He was Abbot of a Celtic Monastery at Penmon in Anglesey (bearing 300°). *Ynys Seiriol* – Puffin Island (bearing 320°) – was named after him.

Higher up the cwm turn left (SE) over a footbridge (2.0km) to critch-cratch 2 (2.1km). Bear S along the wall, across the ancient trackway that connects Anglesey with the Conwy Valley, and up the hill to a Bronze Age stone circle (2.3km). It has been dated at 1560 BC to 1250 BC and when excavated in 1958–9 cremated remains and a decorated urn were found.

Almost 100m to the east is a large circle, *Maeni Hirion*, meaning long stones, dated at 1450 BC to 1400 BC. Maeni Hirion has been misnamed 'Druids Circle'. In fact, it pre-dates the Druids, who arrived with Iron Age invaders, by at least 1,000 years. Excavation revealed a central cist covered with a capstone and containing the cremated remains of a child in a large urn. Nearby were other cremated remains as well as a bronze knife and stone tools. White quarts covered the surface of the circle.

Here is a junction of ancient trackways: from Anglesey and Ireland in the west, from the Conwy Valley in the east, and from the mountainous area in the south. Continue E then NE to a gate on the right (3.3km) and on to a farm cottage, *Bryn Derwydd*, which means hill of the Druids. Follow the track to the second gate (4.0km), 600m beyond Bryn Derwydd, turn right (120°) along the wall to a stile where a farm cottage, Ty'n-y-ffrith, is 100m on the left.

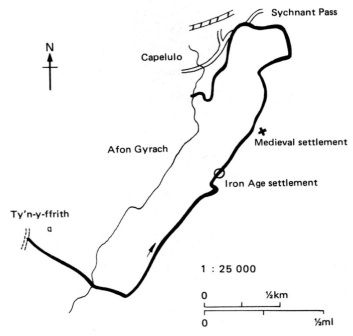

N

Sychnant Pass

Capelulo

Medieval settlement

Afon Gyrach

Iron Age settlement

Ty'n-y-ffrith

1 : 25 000

0    ½km

0    ½ml

Bear 130° to a footbridge which spans the Afon Gyrach (4.6km) and 100° to a field-wall corner. Continue alongside the wall to the ruin of Waen Gyrach on the right (4.8km), turn left (NE) and follow the track over land which is thought to have been extensively ploughed in medieval times, the furrows now lying under the bracken. Descend into a hollow (6.0km) where the track diverges.

Follow the path N, then NE, straddling the route of power lines, to the site of an Iron Age settlement (6.2km, map ref: 746759; elevation: 244m, 800ft). About 2,000 years ago moorland pastoralists lived here in five circular huts whose diameters varied between 5.5m and 10m. The walls were about 1m thick and built of earth and stone. There was also a sub-rectangular hut 6.7m by 4.3m. It was not so much a village as an extended family community.

Through the gated wall opening (6.4km) one passes the site of an early medieval long house on the right (6.6km). There are similar sites further along the track which bears N

then NW. Veering NE to N we cross terrain occupied by hill dwellers until the eighteenth century.

On descending to Sychnant Pass through an iron gate (8.0km) turn left (SW) and follow the path as it winds along the contours of the hills and down to a footbridge which spans the Afon Gyrach (10.0km). To the right, 200m down the lane, is Capelulo.

## Capelulo

This village was born when the road over Sychnant Pass, connecting Conwy to Bangor, was opened in 1772. Eighteenth-century travellers needed such rest and refreshment before ascending or descending the Pass that three inns appeared around the spot where the road crossed the Afon Gyrach. Cottages were built to house servants who worked at the inns, a smithy was established and soon other craftsmen settled here.

But there was a rapid decline when Thomas Telford built the new coast road from Conwy to Bangor, the present

A55, in 1825–6. For half a century Capelulo remained a static backwater – until the late 1870s when the North Wales coast became the destination of Victorian tourists. One popular excursion was a ride by horse and carriage from Llandudno and Colwyn Bay over Sychnant Pass. The cost (in 1905) was 4/6 (22½p), about the same as for a bus excursion in the mid-1950s.

Capelulo, nestling at the foot of the Pass and keeping a respectable distance from its spreading neighbour, Dwygyfylchi, continues to be a tourist attraction. The name means chapel of Ulo. He was a sixth-century saint who presumably found seclusion in this place but there is no church in the village today.


# Dwygyfylchi

This is the name of the parish which includes Penmaenmawr and the area through which this walk has passed. But its practical definition relates to the suburb on the right, covering a triangular tongue of land bounded on the south by the Sychnant Pass road, on the north by the A55, on the east by the promontory of Penmaenbach (030°) and the ancient fortress summit of Allt Wen (050°; elevation: 253m, 829ft).

Dwygyfylchi was old before Penmaenmawr was born. Hywel ap Owain Gwynedd, who died in 1170, wrote in a poem of the "proud towers of Gyfylchi". The Parish Church of St Gwynan dates from the fifteenth century and has been twice rebuilt – in 1760 and 1889.

Follow the lane beyond the footbridge (10.0km) for 200m, turn right (340°) up the track, fork right at 10.5km, then left, and continue westward.

At 11.2km, by the house Pant-y-ffynnon, turn sharp left (150°), then veer right, along the boundary wall, and continue westward to critch-cratch 3 (12.3km) by the Sychnant road. Turn left and continue to Penmaenmawr (13.5km, 8½ml).

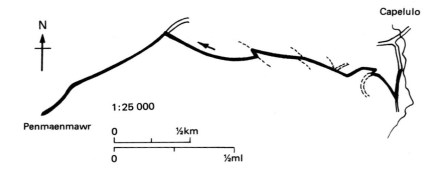

# Llanfairfechan

At least as long ago as the New Stone Age, traders travelling via Anglesey found this a convenient transit point. Whether by boat or on foot across Traeth Lafan – Lavan Sands – the routes E or SE to the Conwy Valley were clear enough. The ancient earthworks, cairns, huts, forts, which can be seen in the locality, testify to the struggles and labours of differing cultures over a very long period of time.

Llanfairfechan was first identified in recorded history in 1253 and in the following centuries it seems to have accumulated slowly round its river mouth until the railway reached the village in the 1840s when it developed as a seaside resort. Now, it provides access southward to the mountains but one distinguishing feature of the village itself is its house names.

*Swn-yr-afon*: sound of the river. *Tan-y-berllan*: under the orchard. *Bryn Awelon*: breezy hill. *Crachan*: shell. *Llwyn Yagaw*: elderberry bush. *Bodafon*: river dwelling. *Carreg-y-ddyfnallt*: stone of the steep hill.

Such apt and attractive names blend admirably with Llanfairfechan's environment.

# Walk 12

Llanfairfechan – Bwlch y Ddeufaen – Ro-wen – Llanfairfechan: 18.2km, 11.4ml.

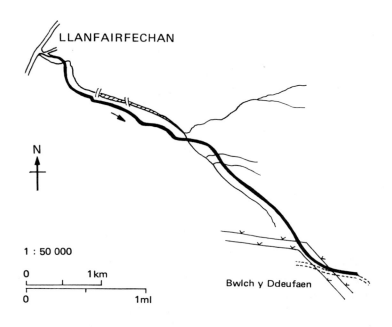

From the Llanfairfechan PO (00km) walk eastward
along the Nant-y-felin road, fork right over the river, known
locally as Carn Mali (0.1km), then left, and continue to a
right turning at 0.9km. Climb the steps (SW) and, at the top,
turn left (E) along the village road.

At critch-cratch 1 (1.4km), fork right (SE) along a farm
drive past *Hengae* – old field – to critch-cratch 2 (1.5km),
and continue alongside the fence on the right (SE) to a gate
(1.7km) and critch-cratch 3 (1.8km). Fork left along the
farm drive, through a gated opening, to critch-cratch 4
(2.3km) and a footbridge spanning the Afon Ddu 100m

further on. Follow the path as it winds south-eastward up the hill and continue to a field wall and critch-cratch 5 (3.6km). Beyond the wall is the open moorland at last! Only the power lines intrude – dominatingly – upon nature's original sculptures.

Bear SE to the near corner pylon of the power line and continue beneath it to a wall stile (5.0km, 3.1ml; elevation: 412m, 1350ft). Near the opposite pylon (S) is a standing stone 2m high. Eighty metres further on (150°) is another standing stone 3m high.

These two stones provide the Pass with its name: Bwlch y Ddeufaen. *Bwlch* means gap, *deu* or *ddeu* two, *maen* or *faen* stone. *Bwlch y Ddeufaen*: gap of the two stones. But these are not the only monuments marking the route of a pre-historic trackway which must have been trodden for countless centuries before Roman engineers used it for their strategic road connecting Canovium (Caerhun) in the Conwy Valley to Segontium (Caernarfon) near the west coast.

Further to the SE is a stone circle known as Cerrig Pryfaid, which may be imagined as referring to stones (cerrig) of the chief bard (map ref: 724713). At 7.2km fork left and, 400m further on, note a large upright stone, about 2.5m high, on the left (map ref: 736717). A few hundred metres down the track is the megalithic burial chamber *Maen-y-Bardd* – the Bard's Stone (8.2km, 5.1ml; elevation: 320m, 1050ft; map ref: 741719).

A superb site above the beautiful Conwy Valley. A place to rest awhile and contemplate how that massive capstone was lodged so neatly upon the four upright stones.

Beyond the cromlech there are two stones (map ref: 742718) in approximate line with Maen-y-Bardd. The larger is just over a metre high and the second, which is about 16m to the west and slightly smaller, now forms part of a field wall.

Continue down the track to the Ro-wen Youth Hostel (9.0km) which is about 1.5km above the village down in the valley.

## Ro–wen

Here was a staging post, presumably, on the Roman road: a pleasant meadow and a sparkling mountain river alive with leaping salmon. Lookouts at Pen-y-gaer, the hilltop fort a short distance to the south, could warn of raiders approaching up the Conwy or from the hills behind. A good place to make camp.

A good place to settle and put down roots. Fertile, sheltered, secluded. *Ro-wen* – the white Ro, meaning pure or clear – suggests its everlasting attraction down the centuries.

Situated in its own attractive cwm, off the beaten track with no through way except for walkers, Ro-wen may look forward confidently to remaining itself.

From the gate opposite the youth hostel bear 030° across the field where Ro-wen appears like a model arranged at the edge of the wide valley. After passing through a gated opening veer left, bearing 340°, up the hill to a field wall and stile (9.7km). About 300m further up the ridge one leaves behind the magnificent panoramic view of the Conwy Valley and looks for the Standing Stone, known as *Maen Penddu* – stone of the black head (10.8km, 6¾ml; map ref: 739736),

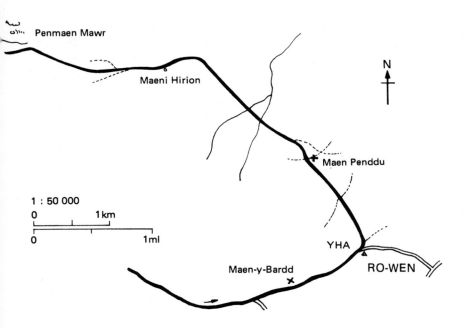

which marks our route as it did those of pre-historic travellers long ago.

From Maen Penddu bear N then NW, across the swampy headwaters of the Afon Gyrach, to the ancient trackway (12.8km) which connects the lower Conwy Valley with Anglesey. Penmaenmawr spreads at the edge of a wide seascape while Ynys Seiriol (Puffin Island, bearing 330°) juts from a corner of Anglesey.

Turn left and continue to the Stone Circle, Maeni Hirion (13.1km), a travellers' rendezvous for about three and a half thousand years. (see Walk 11).

Our route is westward and then NW along the ancient trackway to critch-cratch 6 (15.4km) which is by a quarry road. Turn left and continue for 400m to a grass path which veers right to critch-cratch 7 (16.1km).

Descending, one can enjoy a wonderful view of the Anglesey coast, receding over the horizon towards Amlwch, and into the Menai Straits; and of the near coast, sketching

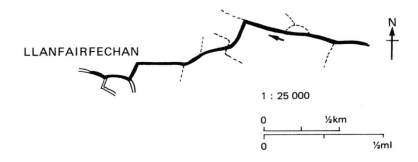

LLANFAIRFECHAN

N

1 : 25 000

0                    ½km

0                              ½ml

the outline of Lavan Sands back to Llanfairfechan, neatly modelled below.

Beyond critch-cratch 8 (16.8km), turn right (W) between farm cottages, continue down to critch-cratch 9 (17.1km) and turn left to critch-cratches 10 and 11 (17.2km). Turn right, down the field through a gated opening, to critch-cratches 12 (17.4km), 13 (17.6km) and continue to Llanfairfechan (18.2km, 11.4ml).

## Aber

Here is a parish rich in historical sites. From the post office and along The Falls road take the second turning left then follow round to the right and you find what is thought to be an eleventh-century Norman earthwork, known as Pen y Mwd. In the early thirteenth century there was a residence of the princes of Gwynedd in Aber and it is thought that this may have been its site.

Across the Afon Aber from the village is the house, Pen-y-bryn, dating from the sixteenth century, and, 500m to the SE, enclosed in woodland, is a hill fort, Maes-y-gaer, field of the fort, whose date is uncertain.

The Parish Church of St Bodfan, which stands apart from the village, 300m to the W, was rebuilt in 1878. A much older church stood on the site now taken up by the cemetery.

If Aber does not wear its history on its sleeve it may be because it prefers to remain a quiet coastal village. The road to the falls is narrow and, in summer, it can be crowded. That is a good reason for climbing out of the valley and up to the ridge.

# Walk 13

Aber – The Falls – Aber; 8.2km, 5.1ml.

From the Aber PO (00km) walk S along the village road for 400m to the second path on the right. Follow this path W for 30m then bear 250° up the hill to stiles at 0.6km and 0.7km. Turn left (SE) along a farm track and continue to a high point 700m further on (elevation: 245m, 800ft).

Here the falls and the valley below have come fully into view and, being above the level of the top of the falls, one can see into the ravine beyond. Several hundred metres upstream from the falls, rising to levels of 535m (1750ft), are extensive pre-historic remains of huts and field systems.

Continue southward then eastward, crossing the *Afon Rhaeadr-bach* – river of the small falls – to the *Afon Rhaeadr-fawr* – river of the big falls (4.8km).

If one arrives in winter or spring, when the river is flowing in volume, the falls appear as a swaying curtain draping the rockface as it drops about 70m (225ft) to the valley floor.

After fording the river the valley path takes one through sites of medieval and pre-historic huts and fields. The main settlement was about 500m downstream where a community lived in rectangular and round huts. A few hundred metres further north there are other sites of circular huts. These settlers cultivated small levelled fields and grazed animals which they would have had to protect from wolves.

On reaching the village road one passes Bont Newydd,

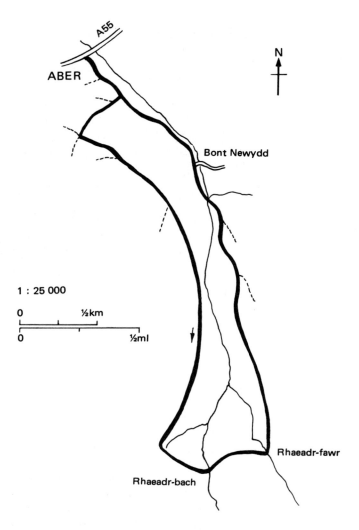

N

ABER

A55

Bont Newydd

1 : 25 000

0          ½km

0                    ½ml

Rhaeadr-fawr

Rhaeadr-bach

an early nineteenth-century single-arched bridge. Stones embedded in the river beneath the bridge indicate that this was a ford for packhorse drivers using the route from Beaumaris in Anglesey, across the Laval Sands and through Aber, to Tal-y-cafn in the Conwy Valley.

## Bethesda

Of all the quarrying areas of North Wales this was where capital and labour were confronted most starkly. Here was the centre of activity of the *North Wales Quarrymen's Union*, and the centre of operation of the Lords Penrhyn, chiefs of the quarry masters.

Richard Pennant, owner of estates, inheritor of Jamaican plantations, became the first Lord Penrhyn and, in 1784, the founder of industrial slate quarrying in the Bethesda area. Similar developments were taking place in Llanberis and were soon to follow in other areas. Thereafter, by means of forced enclosure of common lands, the payment of low wages and a fluctuating but generally expanding market, huge profits were made until well after the mid-nineteenth century.

The Penrhyns maintained a paternalistic, feudal relationship with their workers, an attitude resembling in many respects that of the first Lord Penrhyn to his Jamaican slaves. The workers were objects of Penrhyn charity which was the excuse for not paying wages comparable to rates being received in other quarries. Naturally, this situation aided the rise of trade unionism.

The repeal of the Combination Acts in 1825 had opened the way for the development of worker combinations and, in 1846, a strike was attempted at Penrhyn Quarry but failed. It was not until 1865 that trade union organisation emerged with a fourteen-day strike which was successful in raising wages.

In 1874 the *Society for the Defence of Slate Quarrymen* became the *North Wales Quarrymen's Union*. Quarry proprietors responded by deciding to blacklist every union member. A lockout was followed by a strike which was again successful in raising wages and establishing an agreed code of working conditions. However, these successes were partly due to favourable conditions of trade.

Bethesda had grown with the quarries. It dated from 1820 when it was named after an Independent chapel. At that time it had consisted of an inn and a group of quarrymen's cottages, as well as the chapel. Its population increased with the expansion of the industry and later declined as Welsh slate faced increasing foreign competition and the rise of the tile industry.

At Penrhyn and Dinorwic, the largest slate quarries in the world, peak production was achieved in 1862. In other areas, such as Ffestiniog, output continued to increase until the late 1880s but the general trend throughout the industry in the latter part of the nineteenth century was one of decline.

A parallel trend was the development of trade union organisation. Three-quarters of the NWQU membership were in the Bethesda area, most being employed at Penrhyn and Dinorwic where wages were generally lower and industrial relations worse than elsewhere. Lockouts, strikes and victimisation were prominent features of the industrial scene. In 1885, Lord Penrhyn (Douglas Pennant) repudiated the 1874 agreement, reduced wages and tried to crush the union by blacklisting and dismissing union members. In 1890, annual holidays were abolished and a policy of setting different categories of worker against one other was followed. These actions deteriorated relations still further and there was no improvement in the years down to 1900.

In November of that year a dispute began which lasted three years and may have been the most bitter industrial struggle in British history. It started as a lockout after Lord Penrhyn had instituted legal proceedings against a number of quarrymen for alleged riotous conduct, In response, the quarrymen drew up a list of ten demands which amounted to recognition of their union, an increase in their wages and improved working conditions.

In the following year Lord Penrhyn succeeded in bribing some of the men to return to work by presenting each of them with a gold sovereign. This caused bitterness throughout the district between those who accepted the bribe and their fellow workers who remained loyal to the cause.

Disorder became a common occurrence in Bethesda. The army was called in and the village came under virtual military occupation. Great hardship, including starvation, was experienced by many families. Some had to migrate to other parts of Britain and abroad. At the end of 1903 the men were obliged to return to work because of sheer exhaustion and there was no improvement in their conditions until the First World War.

After the war the union achieved recognition and one of its activities was the education of its younger members at summer schools. When Lord Penrhyn heard of this a Welsh regard for education gained the upper hand and he offered to donate to the union's summer schools a sum of money equal to that which the union itself set aside for the purpose.

But in the following years the cement tile became the main roofing material in building construction as it could be produced more cheaply than slate. This brought slate quarrying to an end as an industry. Dinorwic Quarry closed in 1969. A few hundred men remain employed at Penrhyn which has been taken over by a large construction company. This small-scale operation is likely to continue because roof slates have to be replaced and there is a new demand for slate as a craftwork medium and as a prestige material for featured parts of buildings.

Now, the tense industrial struggles of long ago are part of Bethesda's heritage, together with craft artefacts and artwork engraved on slates.

## Walk 14

Bethesda – Gerlan – Carnedd Llewelyn – Carnedd Dafydd – Llyn Ogwen – Bethesda: 28km, 17½ml.

From the Bethesda PO (00km, elevation: 145m, 475ft) walk SE along the A5 for 100m, turn left into the church-yard, continue past the church to a council road (0.2km), turn right and proceed up the road to Gerlan (1.0km).

## Gerlan

It may appear to be just another part of Bethesda but appearances in this case would be deceptive. Gerlan has its own independent identity firmly fixed in the minds of its residents and friends. It has its own organisations and one of them is called *Cymdeithas Ddiogelu'r Gerlan* – the Society for Protecting Gerlan. A major objective of this society is to raise enough money to buy the old Gerlan School and make it the property of the people of the village. Surely, in this endeavour, Gerlan speaks a homely message to the world at large: that a community must have a school if it is to feel completely itself and be able to look with confidence to its future.

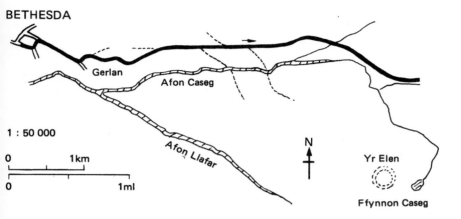

BETHESDA

Gerlan

Afon Caseg

1 : 50 000

Afon Llafar

N

Yr Elen

Ffynnon Caseg

0        1km

0                1ml

About 30m from the village PO there is a left-turning up Morgan Street which leads to a path and critch-cratch 1 (1.2km). Follow the path eastward between field walls to critch-cratch 2 (1.4km) and on to a farm track (1.6km). Veer right and continue along the track to the third gate (2.8km) where the unenclosed cwm of the Afon Caseg extends eastward.

Several streams are crossed before reaching the end of the cwm at about 6.0km where the headwaters of the Afon Caseg drain from a tributary cwm. *Caseg* refers to a mare. The source of the river is *Ffynnon Caseg* – the mare's well – which lies at the bottom of Carnedd Llewelyn's NW face and at the foot of another peak, Yr Elen. Traditionally, it is to this secluded spot that the wild mountain ponies come to foal in spring.

Turn eastward up the stream path of the *Afon Wen* – which refers to a pure or clear river. This is a totally apt name for there can be few greater pleasures than watching the sparkling crystals of the Afon Wen tumbling fresh and cold down the mountainside. On the opposite slope is a traditional mountain sheepwalk, a ffrith, or summer pasture.

After about 500m, leave the stream path and climb the steep bank eastward to the ridge (7.3km, 4.6ml). The ridgeway path extends from Llanfairfechan southward along the backbone of Snowdonia. Turn right and ascend the mound of Foel-grach where there is a mountain refuge hut (7.9km).

Continue S for about 500m then veer to SW and ascend a moon-like landscape strewn with loose rocks to the summit of Carnedd Llewelyn (9.8km, 6.1ml; elevation: 1062m, 3485ft). Which Llewelyn this dome commemorates is uncertain but it is the second highest mountain in England and Wales, after Snowdon, and its neighbour, Carnedd Dafydd, is next highest. Its striking aspect is the view which seems to stretch out to infinity, reducing an immense area to the scope of a single glance. Eastward, the eye leaps over the Conwy Valley and out towards the English border. Nearby, near the SE foot of the mountain, is the lake *Ffynnon Llugwy* – Llugwy well – which, of course, is the source of the Llugwy, the river that flows down through Betws-y-coed to the Conwy. The view of the Llugwy Valley expands as one walks S from the summit, then SW, over a rocky ridge known as Bwlch Cyfryw-drum. One wonders what prehistoric convulsion left these jagged boulders lying in such a variety of prostrate poses.

At Craig Llugwy (11.5km; elevation: 971m, 3185ft), follow the path W, under the crags of Ysgolion Duon, along the edge of Cwmglas Mawr where mist may steam up from the deep valley and dissolve over the ridge. Ahead is the summit of Carnedd Dafydd (13.1km, 8.2ml; elevation: 1044m, 3423ft).

*Carnedd* refers to a cairn. The cairn makers were Bronze Age people and they could not have run short of building material on this rocky mound. Dafydd, the brother of Llewelyn ap Gruffydd, continued armed resistance in this area after his brother's death in 1282 and, presumably, the peak was named after him.

Proceeding SW one overlooks Cwm Lloer with its small lake, *Ffynnon Lloer* – well of the moon, far below. At about 14.8km, the ridge plunges into a very steep descent and when Llyn Ogwen comes into view a truly memorable scene unfolds.

Giant boulders recline in aspects of general disarray leaving an impression of a geological revolution which fled

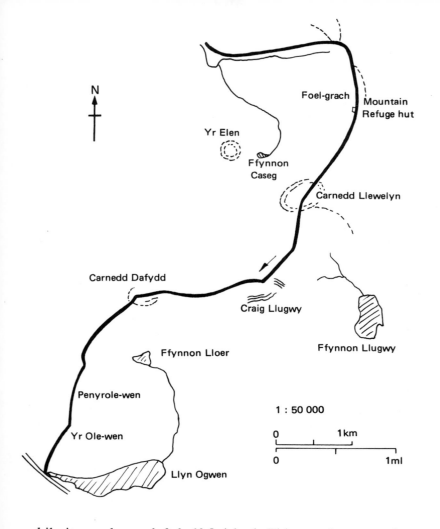

N

Foel-grach
Mountain
Refuge hut

Yr Elen

Ffynnon
Caseg

Carnedd Llewelyn

Carnedd Dafydd

Craig Llugwy

Ffynnon Llugwy

Ffynnon Lloer

Penyrole-wen

Yr Ole-wen

Llyn Ogwen

1 : 50 000

0          1km

0          1ml

while its work was left half finished. This was fortunate for
the practical reason that a descender is offered a multitude
of footholds, handholds and ledges from which to view the
drama that concentrates in this narrow pass.

Ogwen's cold surface turns moist airs into dancing mist
which steams upward, draping the rough crags of the mountains. In late afternoon a fading light from a retreating sun
turns these rugged faces a deep blue. The mist may coagu-

late into a thick white cloud, cloaking Ogwen as the day declines. The heights may remain clear but lower down, if the pass is already enveloped, there is a guide in the sound of a waterfall – Ogwen Falls – which issue the contents of the lake into the extensive Nant Ffrancon. One cannot but feel disappointment at departing from this entrancing scene, sculptured by the retreating glaciers of the Ice Age at least 10,000 years ago.

At the stile by the A5 (18.1km, 11.3ml) turn left along the road then right to the Youth Hostel (18.4km) and to critch-cratch 3. Continue W then northward along what is known as the old Bethesda road. The wide U-shape of the Nant Ffrancon Valley is another example of Ice Age glaciation. When the glacier melted it left behind on the valley floor a lake which was silted up by sediments washed down from the mountains. The glacier also left a great deal of rock debris which was later used in the construction of the A5.

Beyond the farmhouse Blaen-y-nant – end of the nant – and Pentre, there is a path which veers to the right (21.1km). Cross the footbridge that spans the Afon Ogwen and continue to critch-cratch 4 by the A5 opposite the farmhouse Ty Gwyn (21.8km, 13.6ml).

Cross the road and continue on 040° to a field gate. Veer right to a track that bears N up the hill to a boundary gate (22.6km). Rising higher, the valley can be seen extending down to Bangor and the sea. About 500m beyond the boundary gate veer right from the track, bearing 060° then veering to 090°, up the hill to a wall gate (23.3km).

Continue NE for about 100m then veer left to a bearing of 340°, across streams known as Afon Berthen, passing a small plantation on the left. At 24.2km, where the field wall veers left, bear N over the hill and follow the path round the next mound to 24.9km. Turn left (W) and continue down the hill alongside a plantation boundary on the right.

Turn left at 25.2km, right at 25.3km, and continue down to a wall gate (25.5km). Follow the path northward, down through woodland, opposite the bare, blue-grey incisions of Penrhyn Quarry on the left. At 26.1km, turn sharp

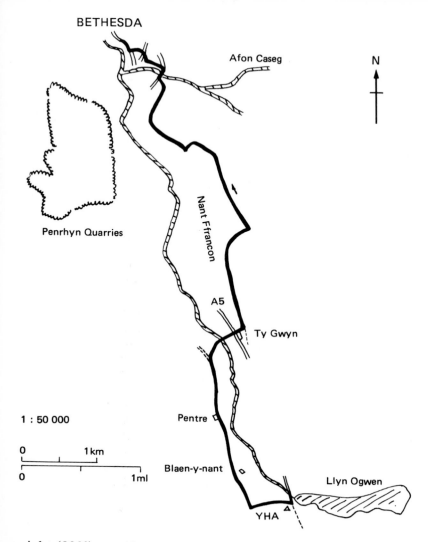

Afon Caseg

N

Penrhyn Quarries

Nant Ffrancon

A5

Ty Gwyn

1 : 50 000

0          1 km

0          1 ml

Pentre

Blaen-y-nant

Llyn Ogwen

YHA

right (030°), continue to critch-cratch 5 (26.8km) and, 100m further on, turn left along a village lane.

Turn right over the road bridge that spans the Afon Caseg, then left into the road Abercaseg, and continue to the lane alongside the school Ysgol Abercaseg. Turn left at the end of the lane to the A5 (27.8km) and right to the Bethesda PO (28km, 17½ml).

# Llanberis

Its origins are as shrouded as its presence can be under a mountain mist. Up towards the ridge which divides this valley from that of Nant-y-Betws to the south there is the site of a pre-historic fort known as Dinas Ty-du (map ref: 567599). One wonders what power was once concentrated here, dominating the Pass, controlling the route between east and west, and how that power dissolved. Near the oval fort are four hut circles (566598). To the west there is the site of a long hut (564598), and to the SE the remains of another (568598). The ancient trackway through the Pass was later used by packhorse drivers, and later still by the builders of the A4086.

*Llanberis* refers to the village or church of St Peris. The medieval Parish Church of St Peris is 3km (2ml) down the road in the village of Nant Peris, otherwise know as Old Llanberis. Between old and new Llanberis there is Dolbadarn Castle, commanding the Pass by the two lakes, Peris and Padarn, truly Welsh in architecture and tradition.

Probably built in the early thirteenth century during the time of Llywelyn Fawr, Prince of Gwynedd (1200–40), the castle was reported to have been used by his grandson, Llywelyn ap Gruffydd, who held his brother, Owain Goch, a prisoner there after defeating him in a battle in 1255.

Another notable prisoner was the Lord Marcher of North Wales, Lord Grey of Ruthin, who, in 1400, had sought to arrest Owain Glyndwr for failing to respond to the king's summons for service against the Scots. In the following year Glyndwr defeated Grey in a battle near Ruthin, captured his enemy and imprisoned him at Dolbadarn.

King Henry IV appointed a distinguished commission to negotiate with Glyndwr about ransom, and, after almost a year, Grey was released by Glyndwr for a sum of ten thousand marks which must have helped considerably to finance the rebel cause.

When Grey left the tower of Dolbadarn he was to become a poor man for life.

# Walk 15

Llanberis – Llyn Cwellyn – Mynydd Mawr – Betws Garmon
– Llanberis: 23km, 14.4ml.

From the Llanberis PO (00km; elevation: 107m, 350ft)
walk S along the main street for 350m, turn right (SW) up
Capel Coch Road and continue, passing the Youth Hostel
(1.0km) on the left, to Tynyraelgerth (3.0km) the last cottage on this side of the Pass. One may be accompanied, on
the other side of the valley, by the Snowdon Mountain Railway locomotive, puffing determinedly on the upgrade or
letting off steam as it descends.

At the top of the Pass (5.5km, 3.4ml; elevation: 473m, 1550ft) turn left through a gate and continue down, crossing the Ranger Youth Hostel to Snowdon path (6.3km), to Bron-y-fedw-isaf (7.0km) and along the farm drive to the A4085. Turn left and, 600m along the road, turn right to critch-cratch 1 by the forestry cottage Planwydd (7.9km).

Beyond the forestry gate fork left (290°) up the field path and into the plantation, left again at 8.5km and continue to the forestry boundary (8.7km). Turn right and follow the boundary for about 700m to the high corner of the plantation. While plodding westward up the ridge one may enjoy Cwellyn as she extends her placid shape far below. *Cawell* is a cradle. *Cawellyn,* or *Cwellyn*: cradle lake. Besides presenting the shape of a traditional cradle, Cwellyn has offered generations of anglers splendid opportunities for fishing.

After Foel Rudd (elevation 572m, 1878ft), a false summit, the path loops westward then northward round the edge of Cwm Planwydd. From the cwm the Afon Goch plunges towards the lake through a rugged ravine at the foot of Craig Cwmbychan which hosts a variety of wild plants that blend delightful aromas in summer.

At the summit of Mynydd Mawr (11.1km, 7.0ml; elevation: 700m, 2290ft) there is a commanding view of the west coast beyond the quarry village of Nantlle and its attractive lake which this mountain helps to supply. To the east, Snowdon, with its south ridge, part of Walk 16, clearly outlined, occupies a central position in a semi-circle of peaks.

Mynydd Mawr is known locally as *elephant mountain* because of the profile it presents when viewed from a distance. The summit cairn represents the high point of an elephant's backbone.

From the summit cairn bear 330°/320° to the edge of Cwm-du, skirt round it NW, N and eastward, down to the mouth of the cwm, then NW alongside a field wall to a gate (13.4km). Here, there is a choice of route. To N and NE, along the edge of the plantation, one can avoid about 600m of main road. Alternatively, bear E, take the second stile and continue through the plantation to the drive of

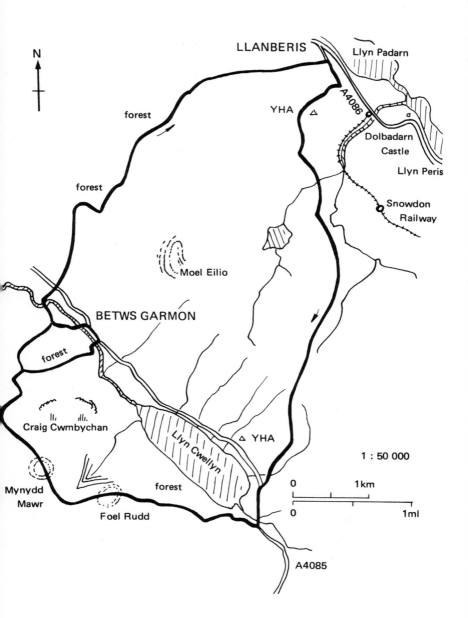

N

LLANBERIS

Llyn Padarn

forest

YHA

A4086

Dolbadarn
Castle

Llyn Peris

Snowdon
Railway

forest

Moel Eilio

BETWS GARMON

forest

Craig Cwmbychan

Llyn Cwellyn

YHA

1 : 50 000

Mynydd
Mawr

forest

0          1km

Foel Rudd

0                    1ml

A4085

93

Cwmbychan farm (14.7km). Turn left (N) to the little stone bridge above the delightful Betws Garmon waterfall which makes up in breadth what it lacks in height.

Along the road is the Betws Garmon PO (15.4km, 9.6ml).


## Betws Garmon

Extending down the valley of the Afon Gwyrfai from Llyn Cwellyn, this was once a favoured retreat for those who wished to escape the advance of the 1831 Methodist revival. Religious fervour had already engulfed Rhyd-ddu, higher up the valley, and Waunfawr, lower down, but in Betws Garmon an individualist could still enjoy his Sunday sport followed by a session at the inn. But when the revival finally arrived, such was its reforming force that the inn was closed and never re-opened.

The Church of St Garmon was re-built in 1841–2, replacing its predecessor which probably dated from the sixteenth century. There is a house, Ystrad (map ref: 541575), dating from the same period. There are also sites of prehistoric huts and enclosures: near Llwynbedw (map ref: 528582) and near Bryn Mair (refs: 513588, 516588).


From the village PO (15.4km) continue NW along the road for 100m to critch-cratch 2, follow the path over the footbridge and turn right. The river path leads to an old bridge that spans the river where it makes an S-bend (16.2km). Turn right, cross the main road to critch-cratch 3 (16.4km), veer right through a gated opening and bear 060°. After about 300m veer to N and continue to a plantation boundary (17.9km) where there is a clear view NW down to Caernarfon and the Straits.

Follow the path E then SE to an exit gate (18.1km), turn left (NE) and continue to the end of the plantation boundary. Veer to N and, when approaching the next plantation, continue NE, parallel with the boundary wall, to critch-cratch 4 (19.9km). This is *Bwlch-y-groes*: pass of the crossing.

Turn right along the quarry road then veer left to a wall gate (20.3km). Bear N but veer NE, then E, down past the quarry pits and heaps of slate waste to Llanberis (23km, 14.4ml).

# Walk 16

Beddgelert – Snowdon – Nantgwynant – Beddgelert: 24km, 15ml.

From the Beddgelert PO (00km; elevation: 46m, 150ft) walk westward along the A4085 for 1km to a turning right onto a farm drive. An alternative exit may be taken 900m from the Beddgelert PO along the Capel Curig road (A498). Turn left (W) onto a path which passes the farmhouse Perthi (1.5km) and continue to the Gwernlas-deg drive. A third exit from the centre of the village through Perthi is now blocked.

Continue past the seventeenth-century farmhouse Gwernlas-deg (1.4km). *Gwern* is a swamp or meadow; *las*, or *glas*, is green, *deg* pleasant. *Gwernlas-deg*: pleasant green meadow. Follow wheeltracks N to a stile (2.8km), continue to a field wall and veer right to another stile (3.9km) where the Snowdon summit bears 042°. This may be taken as a general bearing and one's position along the route can be checked by taking bearings on the two lakes to westward, Llyn-y-gadair and Llyn Cwellyn.

On reaching the path from Rhyd Ddu (6.4km) turn right, leaving the slate debris, and, just beyond a small lake, turn left (N). Now the real climb begins: up the spine of the mountain with an ever-widening view on both sides of the ridge. To the west, beyond the lakes, there is the broad plain sloping away to the Irish Sea. To the east, beyond the mountain's precipitous face, is the depth of Cwm y Llan, receding towards the lakes of Nantgwynant.

One trudges upward, veering NE along Bwlch Main –
Narrow Pass. Here, the weathered crags appear strikingly
stark against a clear sky. In mist, they loom eerily, drawing
one onward by their infinitely diverse shapes that seem suspended in a cloud.

Of course, it is the clear view that one seeks at the
summit (9.5km, 5.9ml; elevation 1085m, 3560ft).

Ignoring the bizarre incongruity of a whistling steam
locomotive, and the jarring intrusion of an 'hotel', this is a
scene of unique grandeur. Here is a panoramic view of
lakes, valleys, summits; all in diverse pattern but orches-
trated to symphonic perfection. What tones to blend the
imagination on such a pinnacle? Should it be from Beeth-
oven or Mozart? Certainly nothing less than the triumphant

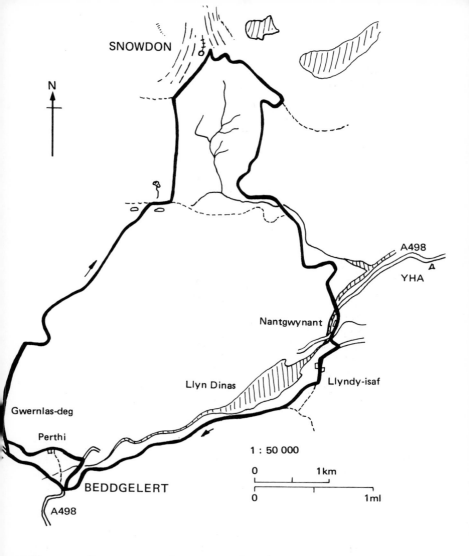

*Egmont Overture* or the romantic *Thirty-Ninth Symphony*. Or, perhaps, *Llwybr y Wyddfa*?

Long before the mountain was called *Snowdon* – from snow hill or dune, it was referred to as *Y Wyddfa* – from *Gwydd fan*, meaning wild place. Can the inspiration of Y Wyddfa be adequately matched except in music or poetry?

Here is an old bard's impression of Eryri, a name that encompasses the random arrays of ridges and summits extending round this premier peak.

Eryri hardd oreurog,
Liwus, wych, lân, laes ei chlôg,
Bur enwog, lwys, bron y glod,
Brenhines bryniau hynod.
Trwy'r hafddydd tywydd tês,
Yn bennoeth, byddi baunes;
A phob gaeaf oeraf fydd,
Tan awyr cei het newydd,
A mantell uwch cafell cwm,
Yn gwrlid fel gwyn garlwm.


Eryri the most spectacular,
Colourful, splendid, pure, cloaked,
Renowned, dignified, worthy of fame,
The queen of remarkable hills.
Through the hot weather of summer,
Bare headed you will be a proud one;
And every cold winter that will be,
Under the sky you will have a new hat,
And a mantle above the sanctuary of the cwm,
As a coverlid like white ermine.


About 200m back along the ridge path from the summit turn eastward down the Watkin path. For almost a thousand feet the descent is steep, then the path gradually broadens, allowing one to concentrate on watching clouds being born.

Pockets of moist air swirl up the deep valley covering the ridge in boiling mist. The wild summit, after venting its anger and sending the new-born cloud on its way, may remain placid for a time, but not for long. Here, moods change with dramatic suddenness.

Further down, one turns east past the rock where William Gladstone, Prime Minister, opened this path in 1892 and named it after its originator, Edward Watkin. A few hundred metres further on the Afon Cwmllan cascades over a succession of waterfalls as it flows down to join the Afon Glaslyn in Nantgwynant.

# Nantgwynant

Arriving on foot at this mountain trackway junction one is part of time and space such as can be equalled in few other places.

Here at the foot of Snowdon the path westward passes the base of the mountain's southern spine to Rhyd-ddu and thence to Caernarfon. To the east, a path meanders round the ridge to that other nodal point, Dolwyddelan. To the south-east, there is a magnificent lakeland trek by Llyn yr Adar down to Tanygrisiau and Blaenau Ffestiniog. Southward, paths wind across to Nantmor and Croesor. A mountain walker faces a challenging variety of routes in Nantgwynant. But the chances are that the village and its surroundings will detain the traveller, for this scenic valley, one of the arterial corridors of Snowdonia, displays real and lasting beauty which calls for imprinting on the memory.

The old packhorse drivers plodded down the trail from the Pass of Llanberis, along the west bank of the Afon Glaslyn, across the river and around the eastern shore of the beautiful Llyn Gwynant, across the Glaslyn again and over the Afon Cwmllan to the point where our path from Snowdon meets the A498 (17.7km).

Follow the road S for 250m, turn left over the river, then right, and continue past the farmhouse Llyndy-isaf (18.8km). The packhorse trail is on the other side of the river, subsumed in the main road, but, returning from Snowdonia's premier peak, one can enjoy the gentle grades of a peaceful lakeside path that skirts the shore of Llyn Dinas and leads down to Beddgelert (24km, 15ml).

# Bibliography

Jenkins, D. E., *Beddgelert: its Facts, Fairies and Folklore, Porthmadoc, 1899.*

Bradley, A. G., *Owen Glyndwr and the last Struggle for Welsh Independence*, Putnam, London, 1902.

Hobley, W., *Hanes Methodistiaeth Arfon*, 1913.

Rowlands, E. D., *Dyffryn Conwy a'r Creuddyn*, Hugh Evans a' i Febion, 1947.

H.M.S.O., *An Inventory of Ancient Monuments in Caernarvonshire, Volume I, 1956; Volume II, 1960.*

Lindsay, J., *A History of the North Wales Slate Industry*, David and Charles, Newton Abbot, 1974.

Roberts, D., *Penmaenmawr History Trail*, 1975.

Winson, J., *The Little Wonder*, Ffestiniog Railway Company and Michael Joseph, 1975.

Davies, G. G., *Gwilym Cowlyd 1828–1904*, Llyfrfa'r M. C. Caernarfon, 1976.

Evans, D., *Bywyd Bob Owen* Gwasg Gwynedd, 1977.

*Ordnance Survey publications.*

# Acknowledgements

I pay my respects to the oral historians, whose recollections about some of the twenty-six towns, villages and locations which lie on these circular walking routes, I am pleased to record; among whom are:

Mrs Jane Evans (Nain), Llanrwst
Dennis Roberts, Penmaenmawr
Harry Owens, Llanrwst
Maldwyn Jones, Llanrwst
David Evans, Llanrwst.

Also to: The Librarians of Gwynedd County Library Service.

By no means least to: Alwena, for reading, researching and evaluating the script.